"Reilly's vibrant, approachable recipes make me want to grab some friends, run to the kitchen, and start cooking! This book will inspire you to live your best life: eating incredible food, laughing with the ones you love, and always adding a little extra twist to everything you cook. Reilly's bright, beautiful recipes are inventive, inviting, and full of joy, and I cannot wait to cook every one!"

—DANNY FREEMAN, author of *Danny Loves Pasta*

"I've watched Reilly bring people together through food for years—online and in real life. Every recipe in this book is full of heart, flavor, and the effortless warmth he's known for. His food always makes it feel like there's a seat at his table, and now there's one for all of us."

—KATE NORKELIUNAS, content creator

"Chef Reilly has created a stunning collection of culinary adventures that gives us all permission to be a little bit extra, both in and out of the kitchen!"

—BEAU CIOLINO, co-creator of Probably This

"I've never been the kind of gal who runs to the kitchen to make a salad, but Chef Reilly and his recipes have me voluntarily washing lettuce. Being extra is a personality trait of mine, and apparently, so is being obsessed with wanting to host dinner parties now."

—CALLIE GULLICKSON, author of *Mocktail Hour*

"In his book, Reilly gently reminds us that we all deserve a little bit extra in life! His bright, inviting, and cozy recipes are my preferred form of self-care."

—DAN PELOSI (AKA GROSSYPELOSI), *New York Times* bestselling author of *Let's Eat*

"For all of us who eat with our imagination first, every page of this book is a sensory feast. Reilly gives comfort food a smart, gutsy glow-up, turning old favorites into new classics."

—CASEY ELSASS, author of *What Can I Bring?*

A LITTLE BIT
EXTRA

A Little Bit Extra

100 Recipes That Serve Up Something Special

Reilly Meehan

Photographs by Erin Scott

UNION SQUARE & CO.
NEW YORK

Union Square & Co.
Hachette Book Group
1290 Avenue of the Americas, New York, NY 10104
unionsquareandco.com
@unionsqandco

First Edition: March 2026

Union Square & Co. is an imprint of Grand Central Publishing, a division of Hachette Book Group, Inc. The Union Square & Co. name and logo are registered trademarks of Hachette Book Group, Inc.

Union Square & Co. books may be purchased in bulk for business, educational, or promotional use. For information, please contact your local bookseller or the Hachette Book Group Special Markets Department at special.markets@hbgusa.com.

Editors: Caitlin Leffel and Amanda Englander
Designer: Renée Bollier
Photographer: Erin Scott
Food and Prop Styling: Jillian Knox
Production Editor: Christina Stambaugh
Production Manager: Terence Campo
Copy Editor: Ivy McFadden

Additional image credits: Shutterstock.com: 22-23, 46-47, 76-77, 100-101, 124, 146-147, 170, 186-187, 208-209, 232-233

Library of Congress Control Number: 2025947495

ISBNs: 978-1-4549-5788-1 (hardcover)
978-1-4549-5789-8 (e-book)

Printed in China

1010

10 9 8 7 6 5 4 3 2 1

This book is dedicated to my parents. Without your nurturing love and empowering trust none of my dreams could have come true. I love you both more than tongue can tell.

CONTENTS

Chef's Story

"THIS PIE HAS A LIL' SOMETHING EXTRA IN IT, I can just tell," the old lady said with a comforting wink. She took it from my hands, passed it to her fellow judge, and handed me a form to fill out.

When I was eleven years old, I won my first cooking competition—a big blue ribbon for my peach pie at the Santa Cruz County Fair (which my dad referred to as the Hillbilly Olympics). My mom drove me to the fairgrounds in our gold minivan while I clutched the pie, still warm and wrapped in a linen kitchen towel. Staring at the lattice top and big, glazed slices of peaches that I'd picked from a knobby tree in our backyard just hours before, I worried over every imperfection. The lattice top was twisted too tightly on one area of the edge; a sloppy egg wash job marred another. Too much sugar sprinkled here, not enough melted butter there. My mom didn't notice those things though—she just told me how proud she was.

I grew up around food. Summer breaks meant working the line at my dad's popular pub, where I would grill hundreds of burgers and drop countless orders of fish and chips in the fryer. I learned the dance of the kitchen at an early age. Okay, it was more of a sweaty, midnight dance-club vibe and less of a sleek modern ballet, but it still set the foundation for my entire career.

Just before I graduated high school, my mom, clocking my potential even before I had, pushed me to enter a competition for hopeful high school students. I had no idea how I would perform, but a drizzle of cherry-infused balsamic reduction helped me win a life-changing scholarship to attend culinary school. "Those are the kinds of touches that will get you far in this industry," I remember the director of the program saying as he handed me my check.

There was no looking back. I started at the Professional Culinary Institute a month after graduating from high school. I quickly found community and camaraderie on the student cooking competition team with my mentor Randy Torres at the helm. Little did I know what the world of competitive cooking, with its emphasis on surgically clean kitchens and jaw-dropping garnishes, had in store.

These cooking competitions took me all over the world to places I couldn't pronounce—from Stavanger to Daejeon—and challenged me to put my culinary skills to the test against some of the world's best up-and-coming chefs. It was a constant battle of one-upping and pushing the boundaries of what food could be—how it could be presented and what flavors could wow panels of expert judges. While I had successes (and just as many failures), my proudest moment was in 2011, when I competed in a mystery basket–style competition in Istanbul. Despite my oven door falling off mid-contest, I became both the youngest and the first American to win the Jeunes Chefs Rôtisseurs competition, hosted by the world-renowned wine and food organization, the Chaîne des Rôtisseurs.

This win led me to a *stage* at the iconic French Laundry in Yountville—and a not-so-iconic eight-hour shift that consisted mostly of picking the woody stems off baby spinach. While this stint was a sign that maybe the Michelin-starred restaurant life wasn't for me, it was a stark reminder that the reason these restaurants succeed—and the reason I had found success up to that point—was because of that attention to detail, those extra touches, that come together to make a dish special.

I settled in San Francisco and started working at The Ritz-Carlton. But as you might have guessed, that wasn't enough for me, so I spent my weekends running a bougie doughnut pop-up. We fried perfectly puffed rounds to order, then stuffed them using specialized caulking guns we had created. The doughnuts were dipped in extravagant glazes, then doused in sweet or savory crumbles and crisps. My doughnut pop-up gave me the outlet to be my extra self, and I could not have had more fun doing it.

I was lucky enough to meet my now-husband, Ryan, in San Francisco. After the first night he stayed over at my cramped apartment, I woke up early, tiptoed around the tiny kitchen, and whipped up a batch of cheddar biscuits. While the biscuits baked, I crisped up thick-cut bacon and fried eggs in the leftover drippings. I whisked up a spicy mayo with sriracha and chopped Fresnos, plunged a French press, and assembled us a seriously extra breakfast biscuit sandwich—all before he even got out of bed.

I tell you this not to brag or prove my worth, but because this book has made me embrace that my life is all about being *extra*, and I hope it can do that for you too! It was never about the trophies, the ribbons, or the praise. It was always about pushing myself to be the best chef and cook I could possibly be.

My life took a drastic shift, as everyone's did, with the onset of the COVID pandemic. While life and work were put on pause, I saw so many friends and family turn to food and cooking to connect and make it through the days. Almost every day, people were asking me for new recipes and inspiration in the kitchen. Ryan and I had found so much comfort in the routine of cooking and eating together, so I began to gather and document everything I was cooking to share and inspire others.

As the world slowly began to reopen, I took a new job as a private chef for clients who allowed me to post the food I cooked for them on my social media. I am fortunate to have gained a group of excited, engaged, and enthusiastic fans who allow me the space to create and experiment.

Being extra is who I am. It's in my DNA. It's in my food. It's in the way I love. And now, it's on every page you will find in here. This book is the next frontier in my mission to get loads of badass bites to food lovers everywhere, and I could not be more excited to share these recipes—some brand new, some passed down from my grandparents, and even one from the First Lady of Nebraska! Thank you for giving me the opportunity to make this happen. I trust you will love each recipe as much as I do.

Chef's Guide to This Book

As mentioned, my goal with *A Little Bit Extra*, and really everything I share online, is to bring as much good food to as many good people as I possibly can. But my other goal is to make you a more competent and comfortable cook and give you permission to be a little extra in the kitchen. Sometimes it's as simple as an unexpected herb or a hit of fresh citrus zest to give a sexy finish to a dish. Sometimes it comes in the form of a sub-recipe you can add if you're feeling the urge to show off. Either way, I hope these recipes leave you with a sense of accomplishment and pride that has you coming back to add your own extra touch each and every time.

In the pages that follow, we will cover recipes from happy hour pairings (you know I had to include some cocktails) to savory sweet treats, and everything in between. There's a heavy emphasis on fresh, punchy flavors and seasonally driven recipes. There are recipes for our breakfast lovers (Cheesy Breakfast Oatmeal, page 141, is a personal favorite), our meal prep queens (you'll wanna make the Black Bean and Plantain Rice Bowl, page 131), and even our hostess with the mostest (might I suggest impressing your guests with the Whole Roasted Tamarind-Glazed Snapper, page 195?). So really, there's a little something for everyone and then some.

I have to admit, I rarely rely on written recipes aside from baking and the occasional cooking competition recipe (where the difference of a gram will affect the outcome), so while I ask you to cook every recipe from this book exactly as written the first time, I also encourage you to lean on your instincts and cook to your own tastes.

Also, please read every recipe from start to finish before diving in. This seems like a no-brainer, but a lot of people don't do it. Understanding the process from start to finish will give you the best shot at success when approaching each cook.

If a recipe gives a time cue, it usually gives a visual one as well, so while the times are a guide, always go with visuals when in doubt. If, for example, you see some garlic starting to brown, but the recipe calls for you to cook it for 3 minutes more, trust yourself instead of burning your food just to run out a timer.

Similarly, cues for heat levels on stoves will vary depending on the type of range you have. Generally speaking, if you want intense color, crusting, searing, and rolling boils, stick to high or medium-high heat. Gentle boils and sautéing of veggies where you may want some color will most likely be done at a medium to medium-high heat. Sweating (cooking without adding color) veggies and simmers are best executed at the medium to medium-low setting. Keeping items hot, or just allowing flavors to meld without expecting much change in viscosity or end product, is a job for low heat. You know your stovetop better than I do! The same goes for your oven, which is why I recommend using an oven-safe probe thermometer in so many recipes—best not to leave anything to chance!

Prep everything according to the recipe's ingredient list *before* you start cooking. In the restaurant world we refer to this as our mise en place, which roughly translates to "everything in its place." If a recipe lists onions and carrots as sliced or diced, cut them *before* you start the cooking process; otherwise, you may fall behind and have less time to focus on executing the recipe and will be forced to . . . gasp . . . multitask! Set yourself up for success!

Recipes that require intricate instructions on how to prepare an ingredient will include them in the procedures. But as a general rule, have everything prepped and ready to go for the most efficient and effective use of your time.

Lastly, I've included markers for allergy and dietary restrictions with every recipe because I want everyone to be able to cook from this book and enjoy it.

- **VEG** means you're in for a vegetarian treat. (A quick note that some VEG recipes include eggs, as well as cheeses that can be made with animal-based rennet. If that isn't your cup of tea, be sure to choose a cheese made without!)
- **V** means it's for all my vegan pals out there.
- **DF** is for those with a dairy intolerance.
- **GF** means you won't find any gluten here, but just a note that some GF recipes do contain options to add on items that contain gluten, so be sure to double check.

Chef's Must-Have Pantry Items

SALT

Show me the kind of salt you cook with and I can tell you a lot about your food. Diamond Crystal kosher salt is the gold standard for day-to-day cooking, and happens to be the only salt you will find in my home. Maldon or other flaky sea salts are best for finishing. French gray salt is a great option to keep on your table, as is pink Himalayan. Please throw out that iodized salt unless it's for craft projects.

BUTTER

High-fat, European-style salted butter is my go-to. Recipes in this book will all simply call for *butter*, so go ahead and cook with whatever butter you please! (I cannot tell you a single time I have used salted butter in place of unsalted and was not pleased with the result.)

OILS

Any recipe in the book that has "olive oil" listed assumes you're using typical, tried-and-true cooking olive oil. If a recipe calls for a finishing drizzle, reach for a good quality extra virgin olive oil, but if you don't have a super-fancy one on hand, don't let that deter you from making the recipe.

The term "neutral oil," which I use in many recipes, refers to any oil with a neutral taste that won't affect the flavor of a dish. Use vegetable, canola, avocado, or peanut oil for these occasions.

Coconut oil and toasted sesame oil are worth having on hand for some occasions, too.

SPICES

Whenever possible, I like to grind whole spices, but for streamlined cooking and easy execution, I'm all for preground spices. Just make sure they're not more than 12 months old. If you need a small quantity, try hitting up a bulk-bin section at the grocery store so you're not stuck with a full jar of something you only use once a year.

FRESH AND DRIED HERBS

You will see fresh herbs called for frequently in this book as they are a chef's secret weapon for giving dishes a pro finish. They will almost always be used at the end of a dish for a bright, punchy flavor. When dried herbs are used, it's usually for a rich, deep, and mellow flavor—think sauces, dressings, and braised items. I love both, but I do not consider fresh and dried interchangeable. I like to store fresh herbs wrapped in damp paper towel, then in a zip-top bag in the crisper drawer. Dried herbs I keep in a cool, dark place in airtight containers for up to 6 months.

CITRUS

I think after cooking a few recipes you'll realize (and side with me on the fact) that citrus juice and zest can be as big of a game changer as salt when it comes to wrapping up a dish and making it pop. I'm never without a full basket of lemons, limes, oranges, grapefruits, and whatever other seasonal citrus I can get my hands on.

VINEGARS

I also lean heavily on vinegar for an unexpected pop. When cooked down, vinegar becomes sweet and tangy, and when used properly to finish, it brings a polished note that is guaranteed to have folks inquiring about secret ingredients. I love vinegar so much, I actually got scolded for using it too much in culinary school. Have I changed my ways? No.

SPICY FINISHES

I keep an array of hot sauces on hand. A few that lean Mexican in flavor and a few more vinegary Southern-style ones will do the trick.

BEANS AND GRAINS

Canned cooked beans (black, cannellini, and chickpeas) are a must. I love being able to cook and flavor beans from dry, but let's face it—it's time consuming! Popping open a can of beans has saved me from ordering takeout more times than I can count.

I recommend keeping quinoa, farro, and a selection of rices on hand. I like to cook a batch of grains to keep in the fridge for quick additions to lunch salads all week.

PICKLES

Homemade jalapeño and red onion pickles are a must in my fridge. Store-bought spicy dill pickles are never far behind. We also love the Mexican-style pickled jalapeño-carrot combo.

Chef's Thoughts on Seasoning

One of the most valuable lessons I can teach you is to season as you go, taste as you cook, and adjust as you need. There are moments where this mantra won't be feasible for obvious reasons (like seasoning a raw chicken breast), but whenever possible, I encourage you to taste along the way and make adjustments.

In professional kitchens we wear coats with pockets sewn into them that can accommodate pens for labeling and spoons for tasting. I cannot tell you how many times I grab that spoon. The more I taste along the way, the more I can adjust and ultimately be satisfied with the final product.

My general rule of thumb when I've reached the final product of a dish and I'm slightly underwhelmed: try a bit more salt, a bit more acid, some fresh herbs, or some citrus zest. Those items, or some combo of them, will generally save any dish you might otherwise find a bit "meh." You will see this instruction in many recipes here.

Chef's Fave Equipment & Tools

KNIVES

When it comes to knives for cooks at home, I always recommend you invest in these three as a starting point:

- **Chef's Knife:** An 8- or 10-inch chef's knife will be your most used. It's good for chopping and mincing and everything in between. German steel is a reliable and approachable start; try Japanese if you're a bit more experienced with knives, as they tend to be a finer blade and require more upkeep. Comfort is king with your chef's knife, so when purchasing, go to a local knife shop or kitchen store and hold a bunch of different options to find what feels best to you.

- **Paring Knife:** Best for small jobs like cutting strawberries, peeling potatoes, or even cutting open containers, the trusty paring knife comes in handy more often than you'd imagine. A 3- to 4-inch blade is ideal here, as you want to hold it tight to your hand to maximize control.

- **Serrated (Bread) Knife:** While a serrated knife is indeed the perfect option for slicing into crusty bread, I also grab it for any task where cutting into a tough exterior leads to a soft interior: pineapples, melons, cakes, and especially tomatoes, just to name a few. I prefer a thinner blade here.

Additional knives I love but don't use nearly as much:

- **Utility Knife:** Something between the chef's knife and the paring knife, I reach for it for fine vegetable cuts or small chopping jobs. It's usually about 5 inches in length with a fairly thin blade.

- **Carving Knife:** A super-sharp carving knife is always great for slicing steaks, chops, or even very finely slicing veggies.

- **Boning Knife:** This book doesn't dabble in much butchery, but if you are cutting up whole chickens at home, this one is a must.

- **Cleaver or Nakiri:** Cleavers are large, rectangular-shape knives often seen in Chinese cooking. They're great for heavy-duty vegetable chopping and meat butchery, but unless you've worked with them before they might feel a bit cumbersome. The nakiri is a smaller knife with a similar rectangular shape. It's a bit easier to use, great for cutting through cases of veggies and very fun to look at, but not necessary unless you prefer it over a classic chef's knife.

CUTTING BOARDS

A good wooden cutting board, like a Boos Block, is my everyday go-to. They come in many cool designs, so they're basically a piece of art you keep on your counter.

Color-coded plastic cutting boards are great to keep on hand for when cutting proteins, raw fruit, or garlic and onions.

A quick safety tip: Always put a wet paper towel or a swatch of rug pad under your cutting board to avoid slippage when cutting!

SPOONS

I think every chef is obsessed with the perfect spoon, and I am no exception. From a great wooden cooking spoon to the perfect plating spoon, I usually head to antique or consignment stores for these. I like wide, deep spoons for plating and serving any saucy dishes, small spoons with a nice well for adding finishing touches like crumbles and cheeses, and a good selection of mismatched silvers is always fun for serving sides and entrées. Trust me, when you pick up the right spoon, you just *know*. Mother's intuition, I suppose.

OFFSET SPATULAS

A wood-handled offset spatula would be next on my list of favorite cooking tools. It's obviously great for frosting cakes and icing cookies, but it also comes in super handy when cooking scallops and fish, or searing small pieces of veggies.

MICROPLANE ZESTER/GRATER

After diving into a few recipes in *A Little Bit Extra*, you'll see how heavily I rely on freshly grated citrus zest and cheese to finish dishes, so best to have one on hand. Don't go crazy—the simplest one at the store is usually the best one.

POTS AND PANS

Having a well-seasoned cast-iron skillet (12 inches or larger is ideal), a heavy-duty Dutch oven, and a few small sauté pans and sauce pots with lids is more than enough for all the recipes in this book. I like an 8- to 10-inch nonstick pan for eggs, cheesy items, or a quick sear on a piece of fish, but if you're well versed with stainless steel, nonstick isn't necessary. If you need a quick refresher on seasoning your cast-iron pan, there are plenty of videos available online. I always tell folks if you dry your pan well after washing it then rub it down (inside and out!) with a neutral oil, it will be ready for use at all times!

BAKING SHEETS

For the recipes in this book, unless the size of the baking sheet is specified in the directions, stick to half or quarter sheets. Half sheets measure 13 × 18 inches, while quarter sheets measure 9 × 13 inches.

PROBE THERMOMETER

An oven-safe probe thermometer is my number one recommendation when cooking proteins.

CAKE TESTER

We use these a lot in professional kitchens to check the cook on blanching vegetables, baked goods, and even meats and seafood. They take a bit of experience to know what to look for when using them, but if you wanna look like a pro, pick one up.

Chef's Thoughts on Substitutions

Undoubtedly the most frequent question I get about my recipes is in regard to substitutions. "Can I use this instead of that?" "Will this work the same as that?" While I wish I had a succinct answer, unfortunately it comes down to case-by-case and frankly, in more cases than not, I just don't know.

If you're swapping for dietary restrictions, I trust you know better than anyone what works for you. Generally speaking, a half cup of milk, cream, or butter can be swapped for vegetarian or vegan versions.

My advice here is you can swap like for like, in the same proportions. For example, switching out half a cup of red wine vinegar for half a cup of apple cider vinegar, while the flavor profiles vary, will generally not affect the outcome of a recipe. However, if you reduce the amount of vinegar by half, you alter the proportions of the recipe and thus risk changing the entire outcome.

That's why I always suggest sticking to these recipes for your first go-through, then adjusting to your palate later. In the end, I have and will always encourage using my recipes as bases to make your own.

Chef's Biggest Tip for Success in the Kitchen

Clean. As. You. Go.

I think when people ask me for my biggest tip for becoming a better chef, they expect me to share some seasoning mix or cooking hack that will take them to the next level. I hate to disappoint you, but my number-one tip for success in the kitchen is a clean workspace. Take breaks as needed throughout prep to wipe down your station, put unused utensils and equipment away, and clear out the sink. Cleaning as you go will give you peace of mind and valuable counter space to fully focus on the task at hand.

HAPPY HOUR

Feeling
a little bit
EXTRA?
Make your own
giardiniera!

The Spicy Gardener

MAKES 1 DRINK

If the dirty martini and the Gibson had a child, it would be this fabulous cocktail. It's classy with a kick from the Ancho Reyes (a poblano chile liqueur) and the pickling liquid provides just enough of the briny flavor that we love from a dirty 'tini. **VEG, V, DF, GF**

2 ounces vodka of your choice
½ ounce dry vermouth
½ ounce Ancho Reyes Verde liqueur
½ ounce pickling liquid from Giardiniera, homemade (recipe follows) or store-bought
Tiny pinch of kosher salt or spritz of saline spray
Giardiniera veggies, homemade (recipe follows) or store-bought, for garnish

In a cocktail shaker, combine the vodka, dry vermouth, Ancho Reyes, pickling liquid, and salt. Add plenty of ice, then shake for 30 to 45 seconds, or until the shaker is frosty and cold to the touch. Strain into a chilled martini glass and garnish with a cocktail pick of assorted giardiniera veggies.

Giardiniera

MAKES 1½ QUARTS

1 small head cauliflower, cut into small florets
2 large carrots, cut into ¼-inch rounds
2 celery stalks, cut into ½-inch pieces
1 green bell pepper, diced into ½-inch pieces
6 garlic cloves, crushed
1½ cups white wine vinegar
½ cup red wine vinegar
1 tablespoon kosher salt
1 tablespoon sugar
1 teaspoon red pepper flakes
1 teaspoon whole black peppercorns
1 teaspoon dried basil
1 teaspoon dried thyme
½ teaspoon celery seed

Place the cauliflower, carrots, celery, bell pepper, and garlic in a large glass jar with a lid and set it aside. In a small pot, combine the vinegars, ½ cup water, salt, sugar, red pepper flakes, peppercorns, basil, thyme, and celery seed, then bring to a boil over high heat. Cook, stirring, until the salt and sugar have dissolved, about 3 to 5 minutes. Carefully pour the marinade over the veggies. Let cool to room temperature, cover with the lid, and refrigerate for 2 days before using, shaking the jar every 8 to 12 hours. The giardiniera will keep in the fridge for up to 2 weeks.

'Tini Thyme Olives

MAKES 3 CUPS

Admittedly, I am not the biggest fan of olives because most people don't show them any love before serving them. But, with the right variety of olives and a fun marinade, they are the perfect snack to put out while sipping your fave 'tini and gossiping with the girlies. These will hold in the fridge for up to a month, so they're the perfect thing to have on hand for unexpected guests. **VEG, V, GF, DF**

- 1 navel orange
- 1 lemon
- 8 to 10 garlic cloves, slightly crushed
- ½ cup extra-virgin olive oil
- 8 to 12 thyme sprigs
- 1 tablespoon whole black peppercorns
- 1 teaspoon red pepper flakes
- 1 teaspoon dried thyme
- 1 pint good-quality mixed olives (like Castelvetrano, Gaeta, Cerignola, etc.), drained

Use a vegetable peeler to peel large strips of zest off the orange and lemon. Place the peels in a small pot, along with the garlic, olive oil, thyme sprigs, peppercorns, red pepper flakes, and dried thyme and mix well to combine. Bring to a simmer over medium heat, then cook, stirring now and then, for about 5 minutes. Remove from the heat and let cool to room temperature.

Place the olives in a clean, dry jar. Pour the marinade over the olives. Seal the jar and shake gently to distribute the marinade evenly, then refrigerate for 12 to 24 hours to let the flavors infuse.

To serve, spoon some olives and marinade into a cute little dish and let them come to room temperature before diving in (the olive oil will solidify in the fridge). Don't forget to put a small dish for pits on the side. The olives will keep in the jar in the fridge for up to a month.

Furikake Party Mix

MAKES 2 QUARTS

Consider yourself warned: One handful of this furikake-studded party mix is sure to lead to many, many more. Perfectly sweet, salty, and packed with umami, furikake is a Japanese seasoning mix made of seaweed, sesame, sugar, and bonito flakes. I've been known to pour myself a bowl of this mix along with a glass of wine and call it dinner on more occasions than I'd like to admit.

---

2 cups Cheez-Its
2 cups pretzels of your choice (I like the windowpane ones)
2 cups Chex cereal
1 cup sesame sticks
1 cup raw peanuts
1 cup raw cashews
½ cup furikake
¼ cup sugar
1 tablespoon gochugaru
1 teaspoon garlic powder
½ cup (1 stick) butter, melted
1 cup wasabi peas

Preheat the oven to 325°F. Line two baking sheets with parchment paper.

In a large bowl, combine the Cheez-Its, pretzels, Chex, sesame sticks, peanuts, cashews, furikake, sugar, gochugaru, and garlic powder. Drizzle with the melted butter, then, using your hands or a wooden spoon, gently mix everything together, ensuring each item is well dispersed and coated evenly.

Divide the mixture evenly between the prepared baking sheets, spreading it into an even layer, and bake for 10 minutes. Stir, then bake for 5 minutes more, until the party mix is super fragrant and a toasty, golden brown all over.

Remove from the oven and let cool completely, about 15 minutes, then sprinkle with the wasabi peas. Store in an airtight container or plastic bag at room temperature for up to 2 weeks.

Thai Lime Gimlet

MAKES 1 DRINK

After the classic Vesper martini, the gimlet has got to be one of my favorite cocktails. Perfectly refreshing, it's a great cocktail to keep in your repertoire as it's easily modified into so many fun variations. Here, using lime leaf gives it a subtle savory note that can't be beat. Thai lime (often called makrut lime) can be found fresh or frozen at most specialty Asian markets. You most likely would recognize the bright, slightly bitter flavor from Thai curries, but I promise it plays well with an aromatic gin. VEG, V, DF, GF

2 ounces gin of your choice
1 ounce fresh lime juice
¾ ounce Thai Lime Leaf Simple Syrup (recipe follows)
1 teaspoon rice vinegar
Thai lime leaf and lime wheel, for garnish

Combine the gin, lime juice, simple syrup, and vinegar in a shaker, then add a generous amount of ice. Shake vigorously for at least 45 seconds to chill, then double strain into a coupe or Nick and Nora glass.

Garnish with a lime leaf and a lime wheel and enjoy immediately.

Thai Lime Leaf Simple Syrup

MAKES ¾ CUP

½ cup sugar
½ cup cold water
3 or 4 Thai lime leaves

Combine all the ingredients in a blender and blend on high speed until the sugar has dissolved. Strain through a fine-mesh sieve into a clean, dry jar, then seal the jar. Store in the fridge for up to 1 week.

Furikake Party Mix, page 27

Radishes with
Butter Brie Spread,
page 32

Dill Vesper Martini

MAKES 1 DRINK

I'll never forget the first Vesper I ever had. It was the refreshing cousin to the martini I never knew I needed, and I adopted it as my favorite cocktail (and, I suppose, a personality trait) instantly! The fresh dill plays so well with the citrusy undertones of the Lillet and the botanicals of the gin. **VEG, V, DF, GF**

2 dill sprigs
1½ ounces botanical gin of your choice
¾ ounce vodka of your choice
½ ounce Lillet Blanc
Lemon twist, for garnish

For a shaken martini: In a shaker, combine 1 dill sprig, the gin, vodka, and Lillet and add plenty of ice. Shake vigorously for at least 45 seconds, then double strain into a chilled martini glass. Garnish with the lemon twist and remaining dill sprig.

For a stirred martini: Place 1 dill sprig in a cocktail stirring glass. Using a muddler, very gently crush the dill to allow it to release its aroma. Add the gin, vodka, Lillet, and plenty of ice. Stir with a cocktail spoon for at least 45 seconds. Double strain into a chilled martini glass and garnish with the lemon twist and remaining dill sprig.

Radishes with Butter Brie Spread

MAKES ABOUT 2 CUPS

Radish + Butter + Salt = Perfection. The French have known that equation forever, so it's time we adopt it ourselves! Here, I've whipped some Brie into the butter for an extra-rich spread that pairs perfectly with the crisp, spicy radishes. **VEG, GF**

- 1 cup (2 sticks) butter, at room temperature
- 1 (4-ounce) wheel Brie cheese, at room temperature cut roughly into 1-inch pieces
- 1 tablespoon honey, plus more for serving
- 1 tablespoon flaky sea salt, plus more for serving
- 1 tablespoon extra-virgin olive oil
- 3 bunches assorted radishes (Easter egg, classic, French breakfast, etc.)

FOR SERVING (OPTIONAL)

- 1 baguette, cut into ½-inch-thick slices
- Fig or savory onion jam

In a food processor, combine the butter, Brie, honey, and flaky salt. Pulse a few times to break everything up, then process just until everything is smooth and well combined, 1 to 2 minutes. (If you want it to be a completely smooth spread, you can remove the rind from the Brie, but I find that wasteful and, frankly, like the bite the rind provides.) Transfer to a shallow serving bowl and spread evenly. Drizzle with olive oil and honey and sprinkle with flaky salt.

Wash the radishes well and trim the tops off, leaving about 1 inch of green still attached. If the radishes are large, cut them in half or quarters. Arrange the radishes on a plate and serve alongside the spread with the baguette and jam, if you like. Leftover spread can be stored in an airtight container in the fridge for 3 to 4 days. Let the spread come to room temperature for at least 30 minutes, or up to 2 hours, before serving.

Spicy Seeded Avocado Dip

MAKES ABOUT 4 CUPS

I'm not here to try to dethrone guacamole as the ultimate avocado-based dip, but I *will* say this dip is like guac's eccentric and fun gay brother—and who doesn't love that?! Each encounter offers something unique and unexpected, and you'll miss it terribly when it's gone. Serve with anything from veggies (dusted with a bit of Tajín!) to toasted pita or tortilla chips. **VEG, V, DF, GF**

3 tablespoons raw pepitas
2 tablespoons white sesame seeds
1 tablespoon coriander seeds
1 tablespoon cumin seeds
4 ripe Hass avocados
1 serrano pepper, finely chopped
1 jalapeño, finely chopped
3 scallions, finely chopped
Zest and juice of 1 lemon
½ teaspoon red pepper flakes
Kosher salt and freshly ground black pepper
Olive oil, for finishing

Place the pepitas, sesame, coriander, and cumin in a small, cold sauté pan (starting the toasting process with a cold pan ensures uniform toasting!). Toast the seeds over medium-low heat, stirring frequently, just until they are super fragrant, taking on a bit of color, and sound like they're popping, 5 to 7 minutes. Transfer the toasted seeds to a plate to cool to room temperature, 5 to 10 minutes.

Halve the avocados and scoop the flesh into a large bowl. Add the toasted seed mix, the serrano, jalapeño, scallions, lemon zest, lemon juice, and red pepper flakes and use a fork to gently mash everything together. I like the play in texture between the seeds and the avocado best when the avocado is not too smooth, so don't go overboard with the fork here. Season the dip with salt and black pepper to taste, then transfer to a serving dish. Drizzle with a good glug of olive oil and serve.

Spicy Blended Mango Margs

MAKES 4 DRINKS

Moving to a house with a pool gave me a new mission in life: create the perfect blended marg for poolside sipping. I'm proud to say this is it. Using frozen mangoes instead of ice creates a thick, creamy drink that doesn't melt too quickly and holds up on the warmest of days. Nothing is sadder than a watery frozen drink. Feel free to tinker with the spice level by adjusting the amount of jalapeño. Or hey, throw in a habanero if you're looking to really spice things up. **VEG, V, DF, GF**

2 tablespoons Tajín, for rimming the glasses
5 lime wedges
8 ounces blanco tequila
3 ounces fresh lime juice
½ jalapeño, sliced and seeded
3 ounces Cointreau or other orange liqueur
1 ounce agave syrup
3 to 4 heaping cups frozen mango chunks (about 12 ounces)

Pour the Tajín onto a small plate. Take 1 lime wedge and run it around the rim of 4 glasses. Dip the rim of each glass into the Tajín to coat, tap it to remove any excess, then set aside.

In a blender, combine the tequila, lime juice, jalapeño, Cointreau, and agave. Add the mango chunks and blend on high just until the beverage is thick and creamy and there are no more chunks of mango, about 1 minute. We like a thick mango marg in our home, but you can add a bit of water (or more tequila—I won't tell) to achieve the consistency you like.

Divide the marg among the four glasses, garnish each with a wedge of lime, and soak up the sun!

Spicy Seeded Avocado Dip, page 33

Gruyère and Parm Cheese Puffs (Gougères)

MAKES ABOUT 30 PUFFS

The gougère is a classic French pastry that you may take some time to become comfortable with making, but once you've nailed it, they're a simple and impressive treat perfect for anything from brunch to happy hour. If you don't have a piping bag with a tip, you can always use a zip-top bag with about ½ inch of one corner cut off to pipe out the batter. I always like to serve gougères with my Jalapeño Pimento Cheese Dip (page 41), because hey, who doesn't love a cheese-on-cheese moment? VEG

- ½ cup whole milk
- 6 tablespoons (¾ stick) butter
- 1 teaspoon kosher salt
- ¾ cup plus 3 tablespoons all-purpose flour
- 4 large eggs
- 1 large egg yolk
- ½ cup freshly grated Parmigiano-Reggiano cheese, plus a bit more for the top
- ½ cup grated Gruyère cheese
- Flaky sea salt

Preheat the oven to 375°F. Line two baking sheets with parchment paper.

In a medium pot, combine the milk, butter, salt, and ½ cup water and bring to a simmer over medium heat. Cook until the butter has melted, then remove from the heat, quickly add the flour, and use a wooden spoon or sturdy rubber spatula to mix vigorously to incorporate it until the batter is very thick and homogeneous.

Return the pot to medium heat and cook, stirring continuously, for 2 minutes. Immediately transfer the batter to the bowl of a stand mixer fitted with the paddle attachment. With the mixer on medium speed, add one egg at a time, beating for at least 45 seconds to fully incorporate the egg after each addition. (This can also be done by hand with a wooden spoon—it just takes a bit more time and effort.) The batter should be thick enough to hold its shape, but not so thick you can't pipe it. With the mixer off, add the grated cheeses, then mix on low speed just to incorporate the cheese, about 1 minute.

Transfer about a third of the mixture to a piping bag fitted with a large round tip. Pipe the mixture onto the prepared baking sheets, piping about 2 tablespoons for each gougère and spacing them at least 1½ inches apart, as they will roughly double in size after baking. Grate a bit more Parmigiano over the top and sprinkle with a bit of flaky sea salt.

Bake the puffs for 20 minutes, then switch the baking sheet positions and bake for 10 to 15 minutes more, until the gougères are well browned and crisp on the outside and hollow but just barely custardy in the middle. Remove from the oven and let cool.

Serve at room temperature or lightly warmed in a cute basket lined with linen. Store leftover gougères in an airtight container or zip-top bag in the freezer for up to 1 month. Just pop them back in a 350°F oven for 5 to 8 minutes before serving.

Gail's Raspberry Ramos Fizz

MAKES 1 DRINK

When my mom was young, she would pick up her friends (and their cute surfer boyfriends) and head up the rugged coast of Northern California to a little town called Pescadero for day trips. She'd drop the boys at the beach to spend the day in the water while she and her gal pals would go to a little dive bar in town known for their Ramos Fizz. I've been to this bar a few times and while I sadly never found any cute surfer boyfriends, I did get introduced to this wonderful cocktail. My riff introduces a bit of raspberry for added tartness and a wonderful pale pink color. **VEG, GF**

3 fresh raspberries, plus more for garnish
1 large pasteurized egg white
2 ounces dry gin
1 ounce fresh lemon juice
¾ ounce simple syrup
¾ ounce half-and-half
½ teaspoon rose water
¼ teaspoon pure vanilla extract
About 2 ounces soda water

Place the 3 raspberries in a cocktail shaker and break them up a bit with a spoon or a muddler. Add the egg white, gin, lemon juice, simple syrup, half-and-half, rose water, and vanilla to the shaker and dry shake (this just means shaking without ice!) for about 45 seconds. Add some ice to the shaker and shake again for 45 seconds more. Double strain into a chilled Collins glass, then top with enough soda to fill the glass. Garnish with a skewer of raspberries before sipping.

Gruyère and Parm Cheese Puffs (Gougères), page 37

Cherry Bourbon Smash, page 42

Jalapeño Pimento Cheese Dip

MAKES 4 CUPS

My mom's best friend, Kim, is the consummate hostess—in a minute's notice she can be whipping up batches of cocktails, plattering poached shrimp, and serving up warm toasted baguette with any number of her signature dips. This dip, inspired by Kim, is now my hosting secret weapon. Whether you're serving it with fresh sourdough bread or crudités, or using it as a spread on a grilled cheese sandwich, I promise it will become an instant go-to in your repertoire. **VEG, GF**

2 tablespoons olive oil
1 small white onion, diced into ¼-inch pieces (about 1½ cups)
1 red bell pepper, diced into ¼-inch pieces
1 jalapeño, minced (remove the seeds and white part if you prefer it less spicy!), plus sliced jalapeño for garnish if desired
4 garlic cloves, minced
1 (8-ounce) package cream cheese, at room temperature
8 ounces extra-sharp cheddar cheese, grated
½ cup mayonnaise
3 or 4 scallions, thinly sliced, plus more for garnish
1 teaspoon garlic powder
1 teaspoon sweet paprika
½ teaspoon onion powder
Kosher salt and freshly ground black pepper
Carrots, celery, pita chips, sliced baguette, and/or my Gruyère and Parm Cheese Puffs (page 37), for serving

In a medium sauté pan, heat the olive oil over medium-high heat until it ripples, then add the onion, bell pepper, and jalapeño. Reduce the heat to medium and cook, stirring frequently, until everything is softened and has begun to take on some good color on the edges, about 5 minutes. Add the garlic and cook for another minute or two just to cook off some of the raw garlic flavor, then remove from the heat and let cool completely.

In a large bowl, mix together the cream cheese, cheddar, mayonnaise, scallions, garlic powder, paprika, onion powder, and salt and black pepper to taste. Add the cooled bell pepper mixture and stir to incorporate everything well.

Garnish with sliced jalapeño, if desired, and more scallions. Serve with plenty of dippables alongside.

Cherry Bourbon Smash

MAKES 1 DRINK

If you are in search of a summery bourbon cocktail, look no further. While frozen cherries work fine, I love to enjoy this drink in the peak of stone fruit season when cherries strike the perfect balance of tart and sweet. Choose a bourbon you'd sip on neat, but not something wildly expensive. **VEG, V, DF, GF**

¼ lemon, cut into 4 slices
3 red cherries, pitted and halved
½ ounce pure maple syrup
2 ounces bourbon of your choice

In a rocks glass, combine the lemon slices, cherries, and maple syrup. Use a muddler to gently crush the fruit and combine it well with the maple syrup. Don't go overboard here; muddle just enough to slightly break everything up and release some juices.

Add a single large ice cube, then top with the bourbon and give it a few stirs before enjoying.

Kimchi Shrimp Cocktail

SERVES 4 TO 6

Nothing makes me quite as happy as the quiet luxury of an immaculately executed shrimp cocktail paired with an ice-cold martini (or the Lemony Cucumber Soju Spritz on page 44 for me, please!). While you could just cook the shrimp in salted water, this flavorful poaching gives the shrimp a hit of extra flavor that takes everything to the next level. Hey, we are a little bit extra around here, aren't we? **DF**

POACHING LIQUID

1 cup dry white wine
2 scallions, cut to 1-inch pieces
1 (3-inch) piece fresh ginger, thinly sliced
Handful of fresh cilantro (about ½ cup packed)
1 small shallot, sliced
1 lemon, sliced into ¼-inch-thick wheels
1 tablespoon kosher salt
1 teaspoon whole black peppercorns
Small pinch of red pepper flakes

KIMCHI COCKTAIL SAUCE

½ cup ketchup
½ cup Heinz chili sauce
¼ cup chopped kimchi, plus 1 tablespoon kimchi juice
2 tablespoons extra hot prepared horseradish
2 tablespoons chopped fresh cilantro
2 teaspoons gochugaru
Juice of ½ lemon
2 teaspoons soy sauce or tamari
1 teaspoon sugar
Kosher salt

2 pounds (10 to 12 count) shrimp, peeled and deveined
Lemon and lime wedges, for garnish

Make the poaching liquid: In a large pot with a lid, combine the wine, scallions, ginger, cilantro, shallot, lemon, salt, peppercorns, red pepper flakes, and 3 quarts water. Bring to a rolling boil over high heat, then reduce the heat to medium-low and simmer for 15 to 20 minutes to infuse all the flavors.

Meanwhile, make the cocktail sauce: In a small bowl, stir together the ketchup, chili sauce, kimchi, kimchi juice, horseradish, cilantro, gochugaru, lemon juice, soy sauce, sugar, and salt to taste until well combined. Taste and adjust the seasoning as needed, then transfer to a serving dish and keep cold until ready to serve. (To make this gluten-free, use tamari instead of soy sauce.)

Return the poaching liquid to a rolling boil over high heat. Carefully add the shrimp to the liquid, cover the pot, and turn off the heat. Let stand for 15 minutes, then transfer the poached shrimp to a large bowl; discard the liquid and the aromatics. Place the shrimp in the fridge until completely chilled, 20 to 30 minutes.

Serve the shrimp with the kimchi cocktail sauce and some lemon and lime wedges alongside for squeezing.

Lemony Cucumber Soju Spritz

MAKES 1 DRINK

If you haven't had soju before, this is a great intro to Korean rice wine. It's low-ish ABV, which makes it a great base for a daytime porch pounder cocktail. Having an elite spritz in your cocktail Rolodex is a must for spring and summer, so I came up with this twist that's basically a pool party in a glass. **VEG, V, DF, GF**

2 ounces soju
½ ounce cucumber vodka
½ ounce fresh lemon juice
3 ounces Prosecco
1 to 2 ounces club soda
2 mint sprigs
2 lemon wheels
2 or 3 strips of cucumber (removed with a vegetable peeler)

In a large wine glass, flute, or goblet, combine the soju, cucumber vodka, and fresh lemon juice. Add plenty of ice and stir with a bar spoon to chill.

Add the Prosecco, top with club soda, and give it another gentle stir. Garnish with the mint sprigs, lemon wheels, and cucumber strips before sippin' away.

Next time you host, set up a spritz bar! Premix the soju, vodka, and lemon juice in a carafe and place it on ice along with the Prosecco and soda. Place bottles of Aperol, Campari, and nonalcoholic aperitifs and juices on ice as well, then arrange some lemon slices and fresh mint next to the glasses for garnish. Let guests make their own spritzes and get creative with unique mixes.

Kimchi Shrimp Cocktail, page 43

SALADS

Crunchy Celery and Peanut Salad

SERVES 4 TO 6

Celery is tragically underrated in my opinion, and I'm putting this recipe out into the world to prove that. Crunchy, spicy, creamy, and unexpected, this salad is simple in execution but complex in flavor. While conventional peanuts work fine, I like to spring for a good-quality Virginia or Spanish peanut.

Serve alongside the Szechuan Steak au Poivre (page 231) for the perfect crisp, refreshing accompaniment. **GF, DF**

DRESSING

¼ cup peanut oil
¼ cup rice vinegar
2 tablespoons smooth peanut butter
1 tablespoon grated fresh ginger
1 tablespoon fish sauce
1 tablespoon honey
Zest and juice of 1 lime
Kosher salt (optional)

SALAD

1 bunch celery
1 red bell pepper, cut into ¼-inch-thick strips
1 cup roasted salted peanuts
1 cup packed fresh cilantro leaves
1 cup packed fresh mint leaves
Kosher salt (optional)
Drizzle of your fave chili crisp (optional, for some heat!)

Make the dressing: In a medium bowl, whisk together the peanut oil, vinegar, peanut butter, ginger, fish sauce, honey, lime zest, and lime juice until well combined. Taste and add a bit of salt as needed—the fish sauce is salty, so the dressing may not require much salt, or any at all.

Make the salad: Save about ½ cup of the tender inner celery leaves to toss into the salad. Trim the celery stalks, then slice them on a 45-degree angle into ¼-inch-thick slices. You can do this by hand or (carefully!) on a mandoline.

In a large bowl, combine the celery, reserved celery leaves, bell pepper, peanuts, cilantro, and mint. Drizzle all the dressing over the top, then toss well to combine. Taste and adjust the seasoning with a bit of salt as needed. Drizzle with a touch of chili crisp, if desired, then serve immediately.

Brocc Wedge Salad

WITH TOASTY SUNFLOWER SEEDS AND BACON

SERVES 4 TO 6

This salad riffs off the classic wedge (an all-time fave of mine) but replaces the typical iceberg lettuce with a quickly blanched wedge of broccoli. It'll make you nostalgic for your favorite red-booth steakhouse while also feeling fresh and new. GF

DRESSING

4 ounces blue cheese, crumbled
½ cup mayonnaise
½ cup sour cream
¼ cup buttermilk
2 tablespoons apple cider vinegar
2 tablespoons thinly sliced fresh chives
1 teaspoon garlic powder
Kosher salt and freshly ground black pepper

SALAD

Kosher salt
2 large broccoli heads, with stems
4 slices bacon, cut into ½-inch-wide pieces
⅓ cup hulled sunflower seeds
Freshly ground black pepper
¼ small red onion, thinly sliced
4 ounces blue cheese, crumbled
¼ cup 1-inch-long sliced fresh chives

Make the dressing: In a large bowl, combine the blue cheese, mayonnaise, sour cream, buttermilk, vinegar, chives, garlic powder, and salt and pepper to taste. Mix until well combined but still somewhat lumpy—don't totally break up the blue cheese. Chill until ready to serve. Can store in an airtight container in the fridge for up to a week.

Make the salad: Bring a large pot of salted water to a boil. Fill a large bowl with ice and water and set it nearby.

Cut each broccoli head into 4 even wedges, slicing them through the stem. (Leave the stem intact so the wedges stay together. If the stems on the broccoli are very long, trim and discard the woody portion.) Carefully lower the broccoli into the boiling water and cook until slightly tender, 3 to 4 minutes, then immediately transfer them to the ice water to stop the cooking. (You want them cooked just enough to still hold their shape and have a bit of a bite.) Drain and pat dry with paper towels.

In a medium skillet, cook the bacon over medium heat, stirring frequently, until crispy, 6 to 8 minutes. When the bacon is almost completely crisp, remove 1 tablespoon of the fat and stir it into the blue cheese dressing. Add the sunflower seeds to the pan with the crispy bacon and reduce the heat to medium-low. Cook until the sunflower seeds are golden brown and fragrant, 3 to 4 minutes. Remove from the heat and season with some salt and pepper.

Place the blanched broccoli wedges on a large serving platter. Dollop the dressing over the broccoli, then scatter the onion, bacon-sunflower seed mix, and crumbled blue cheese over the top. Finish the dish with the chives and serve.

Radicchio Double Down

SERVES 4 TO 6

Some call me the original BGG (Bitter Green Girlie!), so it will come as no surprise that this is my fave salad of the bunch. Incorporating the radicchio in two ways—pickled and raw—this salad lets it shine like a star. The nutty aged Gouda and sweet balsamic reduction provide plush balance for the astringent greens. I will admit it's not for the faint of heart, but true BGGs will fall in love with this salad from the first bite. **VEG, GF**

PICKLED RADICCHIO

2 tablespoons extra-virgin olive oil
1 head radicchio, cut into ribbons
1 small shallot, thinly sliced
½ cup red wine vinegar
2 tablespoons sugar
Kosher salt and freshly ground black pepper

REDUCTION

1 cup white balsamic vinegar
1 tablespoon sugar
½ teaspoon dried thyme or basil

SALAD

1 head radicchio, quartered lengthwise and leaves separated
¼ cup extra-virgin olive oil
Kosher salt and freshly ground black pepper
1 small watermelon radish, thinly sliced
2 to 3 ounces aged Gouda cheese, such as Beemster, cut into ½-inch chunks
Flaky sea salt, for finishing

Make the pickled radicchio: In a large sauté pan, heat the olive oil over medium-high heat until very hot and rippling. Carefully place the radicchio in the pan, followed by the shallot. Cook, undisturbed, until you see a slight bit of browning or charring on the radicchio, about 2 minutes. Stir, then cook, undisturbed, for another minute or so. Reduce the heat to medium, then carefully add the red wine vinegar, sugar, and some kosher salt and pepper and stir to combine.

Cook, stirring frequently, until the radicchio has turned to a beautiful deep purple color and almost all the vinegar has evaporated, about 2 minutes. Remove from the heat and transfer the radicchio to a heatproof bowl. Refrigerate until ready to use.

Make the reduction: In a small saucepan, combine the white balsamic vinegar, sugar, and thyme. Bring to a gentle simmer over medium heat, stirring occasionally, then simmer until the mixture has reduced by about half and thickened slightly, 8 to 10 minutes. Remove from the heat and let cool to room temperature, 10 to 15 minutes. The syrup will thicken as it cools.

Assemble the salad: Place the radicchio in a large bowl, drizzle with the olive oil, and season with a heavy pinch each of kosher salt and pepper. Toss to combine.

Arrange the radicchio leaves on a large serving platter. Scatter the radishes over the radicchio, tucking some of them in neatly. Dot the pickled radicchio around the salad, tucking some in with the radishes and leaving some on top of the radicchio leaves. Sprinkle the Gouda over the salad, then drizzle everything generously with the white balsamic reduction. Finish with some flaky salt and more pepper, then enjoy!

Greek Crunch Salad

WITH CREAMY FETA DRESSING

SERVES 4 TO 6

I like to think of this salad as a Greek-inspired counterpart to a favorite of mine—the classic Tuscan bread salad, panzanella. Texture is king here, so make sure to dress the salad just before you serve it to preserve the crunch of the pita chips. If using a package of romaine hearts, I like to use two; if you're using a loose romaine head, one large one is plenty! I like to serve this salad with my Roasted Chicken with "Under the Chicken" Onion Chutney (page 227) or Spicy Fried Calamari and Zucchini (page 189). VEG

PITA CHIPS

3 large pita breads, cut into 1-inch squares
¼ cup olive oil
1 teaspoon dried oregano
1 teaspoon garlic powder
Kosher salt and freshly ground black pepper

DRESSING

½ cup finely crumbled feta cheese
½ cup plain full-fat Greek yogurt
¼ cup olive oil
¼ cup red wine vinegar
1 teaspoon dried oregano
1 teaspoon garlic powder
Kosher salt and freshly ground black pepper

SALAD

1 small red onion, thinly sliced into half-moons
1 large English cucumber
2 romaine lettuce hearts, cut into 1-inch-wide shreds
1 pint cherry tomatoes, halved
1 green bell pepper, diced into 1-inch pieces
1 cup pitted Kalamata olives
Kosher salt and freshly ground black pepper

Make the pita chips: Preheat the oven to 325°F. Line a baking sheet with aluminum foil or parchment paper.

In a large bowl, combine the pitas, olive oil, oregano, garlic powder, and salt and black pepper to taste. Toss to coat, then spread the pita squares evenly over the baking sheet. Bake until the pita is golden brown and crisp all the way through, 12 to 15 minutes.

Meanwhile, make the dressing: In a small bowl, whisk together the feta, yogurt, oil, vinegar, oregano, garlic powder, and salt and black pepper to taste until well combined and creamy. Taste and adjust the seasoning with more salt and pepper as needed, then refrigerate until you are ready to toss the salad.

Make the salad: Place the onion in a small bowl and add enough water to cover along with a handful of ice cubes. Set aside to soak for 10 to 15 minutes. (This will help get rid of some of the harsh raw onion flavor as well as keep the onion super crisp in the salad.)

Using a vegetable peeler, remove four long strips of skin from the cucumber then cut it in half lengthwise. Then cut the halves into ½-inch-thick half-moons.

Place the lettuce in a large serving bowl, then add the cucumber, tomatoes, bell pepper, and olives. Drain the onions and dry them well, then add them to the bowl. Drizzle the dressing over the salad, using just enough to coat the veggies, then season with salt and black pepper and toss well.

Just before serving, add the pita chips to the salad, then drizzle with a bit more dressing. Toss gently to coat evenly, then serve immediately.

Chilled Beet and Orange Salad

WITH HERBY LIME DRESSING

SERVES 4 TO 6

A perfect pairing for roast chicken or a light fish, this recipe can be simplified by using store-bought, pre-cooked beets for those times when you just don't feel like turning on the oven. The dressing is bright, zingy, and herbaceous; a perfect balance with the earthy beets and creamy queso fresco. Feel free to change up the beet colors or try seasonal oranges like Cara Cara or blood orange. For the perfect pairing, serve it with my Dill Vesper Martini (page 31)! VEG, GF

2 pounds large red beets, greens removed (or about 1 pound store-bought cooked beets)
1 medium shallot, thinly sliced into rings
2 tablespoons red wine vinegar
Kosher salt

DRESSING

½ cup neutral oil
¼ cup olive oil
¼ cup rice vinegar
Zest and juice of 1 lime
2 tablespoons coarsely chopped fresh cilantro
2 tablespoons coarsely chopped fresh dill
1 tablespoon Dijon mustard
1 tablespoon honey
Kosher salt and freshly ground black pepper

SALAD

2 navel oranges
4 ounces queso fresco, crumbled
¼ cup packed fresh cilantro leaves
2 tablespoons chopped fresh dill

Preheat the oven to 400°F.

Individually wrap the beets in aluminum foil, then pop them into the oven. Bake for 40 minutes to 1 hour, until they have some give to them and a knife slides in without any resistance. (The exact cooking time will vary depending on your oven and the size of your beets.) Remove from the oven, but keep them wrapped in the foil. Let them sit at room temperature for about 20 minutes, until cool enough to handle.

Place the shallot in a small bowl, then pour the red wine vinegar over and season with a pinch of salt. Mix well to coat evenly, then refrigerate for at least 30 minutes (they're great if left to sit overnight, too).

Make the dressing: In a blender, combine the neutral oil, olive oil, rice vinegar, lime zest, lime juice, cilantro, dill, mustard, honey, and salt and pepper to taste. Blend on high until you've achieved a smooth, emulsified dressing, 45 to 60 seconds.

Assemble the salad: With a small knife, cut off the top and bottom of each orange, then trim off all the zest and white pith. Slice the oranges into ¼-inch-thick rounds.

Peel the cooled beets and slice them into ¼-inch-thick rounds; if necessary, let cool completely before assembling the salad.

Shingle the sliced beets and oranges over a serving platter. Evenly scatter the shallots, queso fresco, cilantro, and dill over the top. Just before serving, drizzle the dressing over the salad. Store any leftover dressing in a glass jar or other airtight container in the fridge for up to 5 days.

Delicata, Pom, and Goat Cheese Salad

WITH CUMIN YOGURT

SERVES 4 TO 6

I always associate salads with the warmer months—the crisp lettuce, acidic dressings, and seasonal ingredients are the lighter fare we all crave. During the cooler months, I typically just swap out some (or all) of the greenery for hearty roasted veggies for a bulked-up, cozy salad. This recipe does just that. It's studded with caramelized roasted delicata squash, but still has the acidic zing we love about a salad in the form of tangy seasoned yogurt and crumbled goat cheese. VEG, GF

SQUASH

2 large delicata squash, cut into ½-inch-thick rings and seeded
¼ cup olive oil
2 tablespoons pure maple syrup
1 tablespoon dried sage
Kosher salt and freshly ground black pepper

CUMIN YOGURT

1 cup plain full-fat Greek yogurt
Zest and juice of ½ lemon
2 teaspoons ground cumin
1 teaspoon ground coriander
Kosher salt

SALAD

Seeds from 1 pomegranate (about 1 cup)
4 ounces goat cheese, crumbled
½ cup roasted pepitas
½ small red onion, thinly sliced
Fresh tarragon leaves, for garnish

Make the squash: Preheat the oven to 400°F. Line a baking sheet with parchment paper or aluminum foil.

Place the squash rings in a large bowl, then add the olive oil, maple syrup, sage, and salt and pepper to taste and toss until evenly coated. Spread the squash slices in a single layer over the prepared baking sheet and bake for about 20 minutes, until the slices are just tender but not falling apart and have some good caramelization on the edges. Remove from the oven and let cool to room temperature while you make the dressing.

Make the cumin yogurt: In a small bowl, whisk together the yogurt, lemon zest, lemon juice, cumin, coriander, and salt to taste.

Assemble the salad: Arrange the roasted squash slices on a large platter. Sprinkle with the pomegranate seeds, goat cheese, pepitas, and onion, then dollop the yogurt all over. Sprinkle with tarragon and serve immediately.

Broiled Tomato Caesar Salad

SERVES 4 TO 6

This is one of my favorite ways to prepare tomatoes for a summer gathering. The mix of sweet cherry tomatoes with the umami bomb of the warm broiled heirlooms creates heavenly tomato harmony. Plus, who doesn't love Caesar dressing?!

TOMATOES

2 pounds ripe but not soft good-quality vine-ripe or heirloom tomatoes, cut into large chunks or wedges
½ cup Caesar dressing, homemade (recipe follows) or store-bought
5 fresh basil leaves, torn
Kosher salt and freshly ground black pepper
Nonstick cooking spray or olive oil, for greasing

CROUTONS

2 heaping cups torn baguette or good sourdough bread
½ cup olive oil
2 garlic cloves, minced
½ teaspoon garlic powder
Kosher salt and freshly ground pepper
¼ cup freshly grated Parmigiano-Reggiano cheese

SALAD

¼ cup Caesar dressing, homemade (recipe follows) or store-bought
1 cup cherry tomatoes, halved
Torn fresh basil leaves, for finishing

Make the tomatoes: Place the tomatoes in a medium bowl with the dressing, basil, and salt and pepper to taste. Stir to coat the tomatoes. Set aside to marinate at room temperature for at least 1 hour but no more than 3 hours.

Preheat the broiler to high. Line a baking sheet with aluminum foil, then coat with cooking spray.

Evenly arrange the tomatoes on the prepared baking sheet, cut-side up. Drizzle all the marinade from the bowl over the top, then broil for 6 to 10 minutes. The tomatoes should have a good char on them, but retain some bite, so take care not to overcook them to mush (no one wants that!). Remove from the oven and let cool while you prepare the croutons.

Make the croutons: Set the oven temperature to 350°F. Line another baking sheet with foil.

In a large bowl, combine the bread, olive oil, minced garlic, garlic powder, and salt and pepper to taste. Toss to evenly coat. Dump the bread onto the baking sheet, then sprinkle evenly with the cheese. Bake for 10 to 15 minutes, until the croutons are crunchy on the outside but still slightly tender in the middle. Remove from the oven and let cool before assembling the salad.

Assemble the salad: Place the broiled tomatoes on a serving platter, then arrange the croutons on top. Dot the salad with dollops of the Caesar dressing, then add the cherry tomatoes and shower with the basil leaves. Serve at room temperature.

Make your own Caesar dressing—the recipe is on the next page!

Classic Caesar Dressing

MAKES ABOUT 2 CUPS

½ cup red wine vinegar, plus more as needed
¼ cup freshly grated Parmigiano-Reggiano cheese
2 large pasteurized egg yolks
1 (2-ounce) container anchovies packed in oil
Juice of 1 lemon, plus more as needed
2 teaspoons Dijon mustard
2 garlic cloves, peeled
Dash of Worcestershire sauce
1 cup olive oil
¾ cup neutral oil
Kosher salt and freshly ground black pepper

In a blender, combine the vinegar, cheese, egg yolks, anchovies, lemon juice, mustard, garlic, and Worcestershire. Blend on high speed for 30 seconds. Remove the center from the blender top and, with the blender running on medium speed, slowly drizzle in the oils (you can combine them first or add them one by one). When all the oil has been blended in, check the consistency of the dressing. If it is too thick, adjust with more lemon juice or vinegar, or room-temperature water. Taste and season with salt and pepper. Store the dressing in an airtight container in the fridge for up to 1 week.

Grilled Onion and Endives "Fork and Knife" Salad

SERVES 4 TO 6

I drove from Phoenix to Santa Cruz to visit family one Christmas. It's about 12 hours, a bit more given I had the pup in the back seat and had to make a detour to pick up the husband from LAX. We pulled into my parents' house right as my brother was putting the finishing touches on dinner—a crisp and juicy roasted chicken served with a perfectly rustic kale salad. Big chunks of marinated grilled red onions were the star of the salad for me. Partially due to the nostalgia of eating a home-cooked meal at my parents' house, and partially because of how satisfying it was to eat after a long road trip, it's a dish that's stuck with me since first I ate it. This is my riff on that salad. I like to serve this as a big, chunky fork-and-knife salad, but if you want to make it easier to eat, feel free to chop the onions and endive into bite-size pieces before finishing. VEG

DRESSING

½ cup olive oil
⅓ cup red wine vinegar
1 tablespoon loosely packed brown sugar
1 tablespoon whole-grain or stone-ground mustard
1 garlic clove, grated or minced
1 teaspoon smoked paprika
Kosher salt and freshly ground black pepper

1 large red onion, sliced into roughly 1-inch-thick rings

CROUTONS

½ French baguette, torn into 1- to 2-inch chunks
¼ cup olive oil
2 garlic cloves, finely chopped
Kosher salt and freshly ground black pepper

Make the dressing: In a small bowl, whisk together the olive oil, vinegar, sugar, mustard, garlic, paprika, and salt and pepper to taste.

Preheat a grill to medium-high for 10 minutes.

Arrange the onion rings on a baking sheet. (I like to keep the rings intact as whole disks—it's a bit easier to grill them that way!) Brush the onions with a few tablespoons of the dressing or drizzle it over with a spoon. Grill until the onion rings are tender and slightly translucent in the middle and have some nice char marks on them, 3 to 4 minutes per side. (You can also do this on a cast-iron griddle pan over high heat if you don't have a grill.)

Remove the onion rings from the grill and immediately place them back on the baking sheet. Drizzle with about ¼ cup more dressing. Turn to coat them well, then cover tightly with plastic wrap and set aside at room temperature to marinate while you make the croutons.

Make the croutons: In a medium skillet, combine the baguette pieces and olive oil and toss to coat. Cook over medium heat, tossing occasionally, until the bread is just barely starting to get some color, 3 to

Recipe and ingredients continue

SALAD

3 heads red endive, leaves separated
3 heads Belgian endive, leaves separated
1 cup roasted Marcona almonds, coarsely chopped
½ cup shaved Parmigiano-Reggiano cheese
Kosher salt

4 minutes. Add the garlic and cook until the garlic is toasty and fragrant and the bread is golden brown and crisp on the outside but tender in the middle, 3 to 4 minutes more. Remove from the heat.

Assemble the salad: In a large bowl, combine the endive leaves, almonds, cheese, marinated onions, and a hefty pinch of salt. Add the remaining dressing and toss well to coat evenly. Transfer the salad to a serving bowl or platter. Just before serving, add the warm croutons to the top.

Zucchini and Summer Squash

WITH PISTACHIO BASIL DRIZZLE

SERVES 4

When squash and zucchini are at their peak, there's no better way to enjoy them than thinly sliced, raw, and gently dressed. During those moments of peak summer ripeness, this salad is always in heavy rotation at my house. **VEG, GF**

½ cup extra-virgin olive oil
2 garlic cloves, finely minced
1 teaspoon red pepper flakes
½ cup chopped raw pistachios
2 green zucchini (about ½ pound total)
2 yellow summer squash (about ½ pound total)
¼ cup chopped fresh basil
Zest of ½ lemon
Juice of 1 lemon
Kosher salt and freshly ground black pepper
¼ cup shaved Pecorino Romano cheese
Flaky sea salt

In a small saucepan, combine the olive oil, garlic, and red pepper flakes. Let the mixture steep over medium-low heat until it is fragrant and the garlic is just barely starting to turn golden, 3 to 5 minutes. Stir in the pistachios and reduce the heat to low. Toast the pistachios in the oil, stirring occasionally, until the garlic is lightly golden and fragrant and the pistachios have just started to get toasty, 2 to 3 minutes. Remove from the heat and let cool to room temperature, 10 to 15 minutes.

Using a mandoline or a sharp knife, thinly slice the zucchini and summer squash into discs. (Think business card thickness of the slices. Paper-thin slices will get soggy, but if they're too thick, they won't soak up enough dressing.) Arrange the slices on a large serving platter or in a shallow salad bowl.

Add the basil, lemon zest, and lemon juice to the pistachio-oil mixture. Season with kosher salt and pepper, then drizzle the oil mixture over the zucchini and squash. Sprinkle generously with kosher salt and toss well to combine.

Finish the salad by topping with the cheese and a hefty pinch of flaky salt. This dish is best eaten right away, but it's still great after sitting and marinating for a bit!

Crab, Grilled Corn, and Butter Lettuce Salad

WITH AVOCADO

SERVES 4 TO 6

When serving crab, I like to pair it with gentle but exciting flavors—creamy avocado, slightly charred sweet corn, fresh dill, and a bit of spice to the dressing are all great complements without overpowering the delicate flavor of the crab. This salad takes me right to a breezy summer by the pool every time I make it. GF, DF

DRESSING

½ ripe Hass avocado
¼ cup olive oil
¼ cup mayonnaise
¼ cup red wine vinegar
¼ cup fresh dill
½ teaspoon red pepper flakes, plus more as needed
Your fave hot sauce
Kosher salt and freshly ground black pepper

SALAD

2 ears sweet yellow corn, shucked
Olive oil
2 heads butter lettuce, leaves separated and cut or torn into large but manageable pieces
1 cup halved cherry or grape tomatoes
1 pound lump blue or Dungeness crabmeat
1½ Hass avocados, cut into wedges, or 1 recipe Fried Avocado (recipe follows)
¼ cup chopped fresh dill
Kosher salt and freshly ground black pepper

Make the dressing: In a blender or food processor, combine the avocado, olive oil, mayonnaise, vinegar, dill, red pepper flakes, and a few dashes of your fave hot sauce along with a generous pinch of salt and some black pepper. Blend on medium to medium-high speed until smooth and creamy, 30 to 45 seconds. Taste and adjust the seasoning, adding more red pepper flakes or hot sauce, if desired.

Make the salad: Preheat a grill to high for 5 to 10 minutes.

Brush the corn with a bit of olive oil, then grill for 5 to 8 minutes, rotating the ears once the kernels get a nice char and some begin to pop. Transfer to a platter and let cool completely before using a sharp knife to cut the kernels off the cob. (The corn can also be grilled on a cast-iron griddle pan over high heat if you don't have a grill.)

Arrange the lettuce leaves in a large, wide serving bowl, then dollop a few spoonfuls of the dressing on top. Arrange the corn kernels, tomatoes, crabmeat, and avocado wedges over the lettuce, then drizzle with more dressing. Finish with the dill and a sprinkle of salt and black pepper just before serving. Serve the additional dressing on the side or store it in an airtight container in the fridge for up to 1 week.

Fry your avocado—instructions are on page 70!

Fried Avocado

MAKES 12 WEDGES

1 quart neutral oil, for frying
¼ cup all-purpose flour
2 large eggs
1 cup panko breadcrumbs
Kosher salt and freshly ground black pepper
2 ripe Hass avocados, cut into 6 large wedges each
Flaky sea salt

Heat the oil in a medium pot or Dutch oven over medium-high heat until it reaches 350°F. Line a plate with paper towel.

Place the flour in a shallow bowl, then beat the eggs in another shallow bowl. Pour the panko into a third shallow bowl and season with salt and pepper. Dredge each avocado slice in the flour, dusting off any excess, then dip it into the beaten egg. Let any excess egg drip off, then coat the avocado with the panko, pressing the panko gently to adhere well to the avocado.

Working in batches to avoid overcrowding the pot, carefully place the breaded avocado slices into the hot oil. Cook until the avocado slices are golden brown and crispy, 2 to 3 minutes. If the avocado isn't fully submerged in the oil, you may need to flip them over and cook for 1 to 2 minutes more to get them evenly golden all over. Use a slotted spoon to transfer the fried avocado slices to the paper towel–lined plate to drain and sprinkle with flaky salt before serving on top of the salad.

NOTE: If you add the fried avocado, this recipe will no longer be gluten-free.

Bacony Frisée

WITH JAMMY EGGS

SERVES 2 TO 4

When I can find frisée, this is the first thing I want to make. It's super quick and packs tons of flavor into minimal ingredients. When serving, make sure the eggs and the dressing are still slightly warm. When contrasted with the cool, crisp frisée, it creates something special. I like to serve it with some crusty baguette and Brie cheese or a nice pasta dish like the DBG Rotini (page 104). GF, DF

---

1 teaspoon baking soda
3 high-quality large eggs
4 slices thick-cut bacon, cut into 1-inch pieces
1 medium shallot, finely diced
2 garlic cloves, finely diced
¼ cup sherry vinegar
2 tablespoons olive oil
1 tablespoon stone-ground or whole-grain mustard
1 teaspoon sugar or honey
Kosher salt and freshly ground black pepper
2 or 3 heads frisée, cut into 1- to 2-inch pieces (4 to 6 cups)
3 or 4 French breakfast radishes, thinly sliced

Bring a medium saucepan of water to a rolling boil over high heat. Once the water boils, sprinkle in the baking soda (this makes the cooked eggs easier to peel). Carefully add the eggs and cook them for exactly 6 minutes, maintaining the rolling boil for the entire cook time. (This will give you the perfect runny center.) Drain the eggs, then roll them around in the pan to crack the shells a bit. Run the eggs under cold water for about 30 seconds, then peel them.

Place the bacon in a cold large skillet. Cook over medium heat, stirring frequently, until crisp and browned, 8 to 10 minutes. Transfer the bacon to a paper towel–lined plate to drain, leaving all the fat behind in the pan.

In the pan with the bacon grease, combine the shallot and garlic and cook over medium-low heat just until softened and fragrant, 2 to 3 minutes. Turn off the heat, then whisk in the vinegar, olive oil, mustard, and sugar. Season with salt and pepper and keep the dressing warm until ready to serve.

Arrange the bacon and frisée together in a shallow bowl or on a serving platter, then sprinkle the radishes over the top. Drizzle the dressing all over. Cut the eggs in half and season with salt and pepper, then tuck them into the frisée and serve immediately.

Kale Chip Salad

SERVES 4 TO 6

You all know how much I love to layer textures in my dishes. The kale chips take an otherwise simple salad to the next level by adding a fun, shatteringly crisp element. Don't limit yourself to putting them on this salad! They're great on pasta dishes, on top of a piece of fish, or just for snacking. Make sure to top the salad with the chips *just* before you serve the salad to avoid sogginess. **VEG, GF**

KALE CHIPS

Nonstick cooking spray
1 bunch lacinato kale, leaves stemmed
1 small block Parmigiano-Reggiano cheese
Kosher salt

DRESSING

¼ cup neutral oil
¼ cup plain full-fat Greek yogurt
Zest of ½ lemon
Juice of 1 large lemon
1 or 2 garlic cloves, grated or minced
1 teaspoon garlic powder
Kosher salt and freshly ground black pepper

SALAD

1 bunch lacinato kale, leaves stemmed and cut into ½-inch-thick ribbons
1 medium head red-leaf lettuce, leaves cut or torn into 1- to 2-inch pieces
1½ cups quartered red grapes

Make the kale chips: Preheat the oven to 315°F. Line two baking sheets with aluminum foil, then lightly coat with cooking spray.

Arrange the kale leaves on the prepared baking sheets. Evenly coat each leaf with cooking spray, then grate 2 to 3 tablespoons of the cheese directly over the kale in an even layer. Season with a hefty pinch of salt, then bake for 20 to 25 minutes, until the kale is crispy all over and the edges are lightly browned. Remove from the oven and let cool completely.

Make the dressing: In a small bowl, whisk together the oil, yogurt, lemon zest, lemon juice, garlic, garlic powder, and salt and pepper to taste. Mix thoroughly, then taste and adjust the seasoning. Refrigerate until you're ready to toss the salad.

Assemble the salad: Combine the kale ribbons and lettuce in a large bowl. Top the greens mixture with the grapes, then season with salt and pepper, add all the dressing, and toss well. Transfer to a large, shallow serving bowl. Just before serving, top with the crisp kale chips.

SOUPS & STEWS

Gingery Pork Meatballs and Noodles

WITH BOK CHOY AND TOASTY GARLIC DRIZZLE

SERVES 4

This light, brothy soup is a comfort classic for me when I'm feeling a bit under the weather or just craving something with a delicious gingery kick. The meatballs are tender and moist, given they are barely bound together by egg white and cornstarch, and the crispy garlic drizzle lusciously coats each noodle as you slurp away—make extra drizzle because you'll want to put it on everything. I like to cook the noodles separately in salted water as you can control the cook time on everything more accurately, and you're not adding any starch to the broth of the soup, which will change the consistency. Plus, if you have any leftovers, the noodles don't get soggy for the next day! DF

GARLIC OIL DRIZZLE

¼ cup neutral oil
2 teaspoons toasted sesame oil
3 garlic cloves, grated or minced
1 tablespoon white sesame seeds
3 scallions, green parts only, very thinly sliced
1 teaspoon kosher salt

MEATBALLS

1 pound ground pork
1 large egg white
3 scallions, white parts only, minced
1 tablespoon cornstarch
1 tablespoon grated fresh ginger
1 tablespoon low-sodium soy sauce
1 tablespoon rice vinegar
2 teaspoons kosher salt

Make the drizzle: In a small saucepan, heat the neutral oil and sesame oil over medium heat. Stir in the garlic and sesame seeds and cook until fragrant and the garlic is just beginning to take on color, 2 to 3 minutes, then immediately remove from the heat. (Keep an eye on the garlic, as it can turn dark and bitter quickly.) Stir in the scallion greens and the salt—take care, as it will bubble up in the hot oil.

Make the meatballs: In a large bowl, combine the pork, egg white, scallion whites, cornstarch, ginger, soy sauce, vinegar, and salt. Mix well with chopsticks or a spoon and ensure everything is evenly distributed. Refrigerate the meat mixture while you make the soup.

Make the soup: In a large pot or Dutch oven, heat the neutral oil over medium heat. Add the onion and ginger and cook until the onion is soft and translucent and the ginger is fragrant, 3 to 4 minutes. (You don't want them to take on any color, so if they start to brown, reduce the heat.) Add the mushrooms, then pour in the stock, soy sauce, and sugar and stir well. Give it a taste and sason with salt to your liking. Bring the soup to a low simmer and cook until the flavors have melded, about 15 minutes.

Meanwhile, bring a medium pot of salted water to a boil over high heat.

Ensure the soup is at a simmer (not a boil, or the meatballs will be tough or

Recipe and ingredients continue

SOUP

2 tablespoons neutral oil
½ small yellow onion, sliced into thin strips
1 tablespoon coarsely chopped fresh ginger
2 ounces fresh shiitake mushrooms, stemmed and thinly sliced
6 cups chicken stock or pork stock
2 to 3 tablespoons low-sodium soy sauce
1 tablespoon sugar
Kosher salt
6 to 8 ounces ramen or udon noodles, for serving
3 small heads baby bok choy, leaves separated
Togarashi seasoning, for garnish (optional)

fall apart). Use a cookie scoop or two spoons to shape the meat mixture into 1-inch balls, then carefully drop them right into the simmering soup (you should end up with 16 to 20 meatballs). Cook, stirring occasionally, until the meatballs are cooked through, 10 to 12 minutes. They will go from pink to a light gray all the way through when fully cooked.

Drop the noodles into the pot of boiling water and cook them according to the package directions, then drain. Divide the noodles among four individual serving bowls.

Gently stir the bok choy into the soup. Simmer until the bok choy leaves are tender but the white cores still have a bit of a bite to them, about 2 minutes. Ladle the soup into the bowls with the cooked noodles, evenly dividing the meatballs and bok choy among them. Drizzle each bowl generously with the garlic oil, sprinkle with togarashi, if you like, and enjoy!

Silky Gochujang Butternut Soup

WITH SESAME BEAN SPROUTS

SERVES 4 TO 6

Living in San Francisco introduced me to the wonders of Korean food—banchan specifically—and it has remained one of my favorite cuisines to date. One restaurant I frequented served a small dish of ice-cold, supremely spicy marinated cubes of butternut squash tossed with crisp bean sprouts that had been gently bathed in a salty sesame dressing. Naturally, the chilly SF nights inspired me to turn that dish into a comfy bowl of soup. If you aren't already familiar with the Korean fermented chile paste gochujang, you'll love its pleasant spice and complex umami finish. VEG, V, DF

SOUP

2 pounds butternut squash (about 2 small or 1 large), peeled and diced into 1-inch pieces
4 tablespoons olive oil
1 tablespoon pure maple syrup
1 teaspoon toasted sesame oil
Kosher salt
1 small sweet onion, diced into 1-inch pieces
1 tablespoon minced fresh ginger
3 or 4 garlic cloves, minced
2 scallions, white parts only, minced
2 to 3 tablespoons gochujang
4 cups vegetable stock
Freshly ground black pepper

BEAN SPROUTS

Large handful of mung bean sprouts (about 2 cups)
2 scallions, green parts only, very thinly sliced
1 tablespoon neutral oil
1 tablespoon white sesame seeds, toasted
1 teaspoon toasted sesame oil
1 teaspoon sugar
1 teaspoon light soy sauce
Kosher salt

Make the soup: Preheat the oven to 400°F. Line a baking sheet with parchment paper or aluminum foil.

In a large bowl, toss the butternut squash with 2 tablespoons of the olive oil, the maple syrup, and the sesame oil until evenly coated. Season with a heavy pinch of salt, then spread the squash on the prepared baking sheet in a single layer. Roast for 20 to 25 minutes, until fork-tender and slightly caramelized.

Meanwhile, in a large Dutch oven or pot, heat the remaining 2 tablespoons olive oil over medium heat. Add the onion and cook until it has softened a bit and just begun to take on some light browning on the edges, 5 to 7 minutes. Stir in the ginger, garlic, and scallions and cook until super fragrant, 2 to 3 minutes more. Add the gochujang and cook, stirring continuously, for about 1 minute, just to lightly toast it and coat all the onions. Immediately add the stock and stir, scraping up any browned bits stuck to the bottom of the pot.

When the squash is done, add it to the pot and stir well to combine. Bring the mixture to a simmer and cook until the flavors have melded and the squash is starting to fall apart, 15 to 20 minutes.

Meanwhile, make the bean sprouts: In a small bowl, combine the bean sprouts, scallions, neutral oil, sesame seeds, sesame oil, sugar, and soy sauce and toss to coat. Season with salt to taste, then let marinate at room temperature while you finish the soup.

Recipe continues

NOTE: Hot liquids are best blended in small batches with an escape route for steam! If your blender has a removable piece, take it off and cover it with a kitchen towel before blending, if not, just be sure to fill your blender less than halfway. Always start at the lowest setting and work your way up to higher ones. An immersion blender can be used in place of a regular blender but may not result in a soup quite as smooth.

Remove the pot from heat. Using an immersion blender, blend the soup until smooth. (Alternatively, working in batches, carefully transfer to a standing blender and blend until smooth. Take care to never fill the blender more than halfway full with hot liquid, and crack the lid or it may explode!)

Taste the soup and season with salt and pepper as needed, then ladle it into bowls. Top with a generous mound of the marinated bean sprouts and serve immediately.

Cannellini Bean and Potato Stew

WITH BROCCOLI RABE

SERVES 4 TO 6

The best way to complement bitter greens—like broccoli rabe here—is with something creamy and something acidic. The Yukon Golds and cannellini beans cook down to perfectly fluffy additions that coat the broccoli rabe, while the lemon rounds it all out and gives this hearty veggie stew a bright boost that amplifies the rest of the flavors. **GF, DF**

8 ounces diced pancetta
1 medium yellow onion, diced into ¼-inch pieces
6 garlic cloves, very thinly sliced
1 large Yukon Gold potato, diced into ½-inch pieces (about 1½ cups)
2 (15-ounce) cans cannellini beans, drained and rinsed
6 cups chicken stock or vegetable stock
2 teaspoons garlic powder
1 teaspoon dried basil or thyme
1 teaspoon red pepper flakes
Kosher salt and freshly ground black pepper
1 bunch broccoli rabe, bottom inch trimmed, cut into roughly 1-inch pieces
Zest and juice of 1 lemon
Crusty bread, for serving (optional)

In a large pot or Dutch oven, cook the pancetta over medium heat, stirring frequently, until it begins to render its fat and turn golden brown, about 5 minutes. Add the onion to the pot and cook until softened, translucent, and just browning on the edges, 3 to 4 minutes. Add the garlic and cook until fragrant, 1 to 2 minutes. Add the potato to the pot and stir to combine. Cook for 4 to 5 minutes, until they begin to turn translucent, then add the beans.

Pour in the stock and bring the mixture to a boil over medium-high heat. Season the soup with the garlic powder, basil, red pepper flakes, a hefty pinch of salt, and some black pepper, then reduce the heat to low. Simmer gently until the potatoes are tender when you bite into them but not falling apart, 15 to 20 minutes.

Stir in the broccoli rabe and cook until the stalks are tender but still a vibrant green, 3 to 5 minutes.

Right before serving, stir in the lemon zest (reserving some for garnish) and juice. Taste and adjust the seasoning as needed, then ladle the soup into bowls, top with remaining lemon zest, and serve with crusty bread for dipping.

Seabright Seafood Bisque

SERVES 4 TO 6

My dad owned a pub called the Seabright Brewery when I was growing up, which is where I fell in love with food and got my start in the kitchen. While the dishes were simple pub fare, there was an emphasis on quality ingredients. Our seafood bisque used the freshest seafood available in a rich, tomatoey broth; it kept regulars coming back for decades. Before you say it, I am fully aware this is not a traditional bisque by any means. But for the sake of nostalgia, I just couldn't bring myself to change the name. Feel free to swap the salmon or scallops for any hearty fresh-looking fish—just stick to the weights provided for best results! The key to this dish is cooking the seafood perfectly, then serving it immediately. So once the seafood is added, pay close attention. No shame in cracking open a scallop or chunk of salmon to check the cook!

---

2 tablespoons olive oil
2 tablespoons butter
1 small yellow onion, diced small
1 small fennel bulb, finely diced
2 or 3 garlic cloves, minced
2 tablespoons tomato paste
2 teaspoons sweet paprika
1 teaspoon dried oregano
1 teaspoon garlic powder
2 tablespoons all-purpose flour
1 cup dry white wine
4 cups seafood stock or chicken stock
1 (14-ounce) can chopped tomatoes, with their liquid
Kosher salt
1 pound (16 to 20 count) shrimp, peeled, deveined, and cut into 1-inch pieces
1 (6.5-ounce) can chopped clams with their liquid
1 pound salmon fillet, skin removed, diced into 1-inch pieces
½ pound small scallops, cut in half
½ cup heavy cream
¼ cup chopped fresh parsley
Warmed sourdough bread, for serving

In a large pot or Dutch oven, heat the olive oil and butter over medium heat. When the butter has melted, add the onion and fennel. Cook, stirring frequently, until softened and translucent but not browned at all, about 5 minutes. Add the garlic and cook, stirring frequently, for another minute. Stir in the tomato paste, paprika, oregano, and garlic powder and cook until the spices begin to bloom and the raw tomato paste taste has dissipated, about 2 minutes.

Sprinkle the flour over the vegetables and stir well to combine. Cook, stirring frequently, until the roux is fragrant and nutty and has begun to stick to the bottom of the pot, 2 to 3 minutes. While stirring continuously, pour in the wine, being sure to scrape up any of the flour and tomato paste stuck to the bottom of the pot. Cook for about 2 minutes to cook off the wine. The mixture will be very thick.

Carefully pour in the stock and tomatoes and their liquid, and stir to combine. Add a bit of salt, then reduce the heat to medium-low and bring the bisque base to a low simmer. Cover and cook, stirring occasionally, so all the flavors can meld, 20 to 25 minutes.

Remove the "foot" (small side muscle) from the scallops if it's present. Add the shrimp, clams and their liquid, salmon, and scallops and give the soup a gentle stir so all the seafood is submerged. Cook until the seafood is just cooked through, 5 to 7 minutes.

When the seafood is almost totally cooked, stir in the cream and cook just until the bisque is heated through, 2 to 3 minutes more, then stir in the parsley. Taste and adjust the seasoning with salt as needed.

Ladle the bisque into serving bowls and serve with some warm sourdough bread alongside for dunking.

Creamy Vidalia Onion Soup

WITH GOAT CHEESE TOASTS AND POMEGRANATE

SERVES 4 TO 6

This is a dish I created while working at The Bohemian Club in San Francisco. It quickly became a hit with the club's members and was a staple at events during the winter months. It's easy to see why: The tangy goat cheese and creamy, sweet onion flavor meld into a velvety soup that's basically a cashmere sweater in a bowl. The unexpected pop of tart pomegranate creates a wonderful balance. **VEG**

SOUP

½ cup (1 stick) butter
2 pounds Vidalia onions, thinly sliced
3 garlic cloves, finely chopped
6 to 8 thyme sprigs
2 tablespoons all-purpose flour
¼ cup apple cider vinegar
4 cups vegetable stock
½ cup heavy cream
Kosher salt

TOASTS

4 ounces goat cheese, at room temperature
2 teaspoons olive oil, plus more for brushing
1 teaspoon apple cider vinegar
1 teaspoon chopped fresh thyme
Kosher salt and freshly ground black pepper
1 French or sourdough baguette, cut on a 45-degree angle into ½-inch-thick slices

About ½ cup cleaned pomegranate seeds, for garnish
Extra-virgin olive oil, for garnish
Fresh thyme leaves, for garnish

Make the soup: In a large pot or Dutch oven, melt the butter over medium heat. Add the onions and cook, stirring frequently to avoid any dark spots, until lightly caramelized (think the color of an iced latte), 20 to 25 minutes. Add the garlic and thyme and cook for 3 to 4 minutes more to remove the raw garlic taste.

Sprinkle the flour over the onions and stir well to coat. Cook for 2 to 3 minutes, then pour in the vinegar and stir, scraping up any browned bits from the bottom of the pot. Pour in the stock, stirring to combine and break up all the flour so it doesn't clump. Increase the heat to medium-high and bring the mixture to a boil, then reduce the heat to medium-low and cook uncovered, stirring occasionally, 15 to 20 minutes to allow the flavors to meld. Turn off the heat, remove the thyme sprigs, stir in the cream, and add kosher salt to taste.

Using an immersion blender, blend the soup directly in the pot until silky-smooth. (Alternatively, carefully transfer the soup to a standing blender and blend on high until smooth, then return the soup to the pot. See page 82 for safe blending instructions.) Keep the soup hot over low heat.

Make the toasts: Preheat the oven to 375°F. Line a baking sheet with parchment paper or aluminum foil.

In a small bowl, mix together the cheese, olive oil, vinegar, thyme, and some salt and pepper until well combined.

Place the baguette slices on the prepared baking sheet and brush each lightly with oil. Spread a generous amount of the goat cheese mixture onto each slice, then bake for 10 to 12 minutes, until the edges are golden and the cheese is melted and slightly bubbly.

Ladle the soup into bowls. Sprinkle each bowl with some pomegranate seeds and a bit of pepper, and finish with a light drizzle of olive oil and some fresh thyme leaves just before digging in. Serve each bowl of soup with 1 or 2 cheese toasts.

Ryan's "Famous" Kale and Mushie Soup

WITH CHEESY TORTELLINI

SERVES 4 TO 6

It will come as no surprise that I do the majority of the cooking in our household—but even so, this recipe of Ryan's is one we find ourselves making over and over again. It's cozy and rich without being heavy, and the added little splash of red wine vinegar at the end puts a bow on top. While Ryan prefers to cook the tortellini on the side, then add them right before digging in, I like to cook them in the broth so they soak up all the flavor we worked so hard to develop—the choice is up to you.

---

2 tablespoons olive oil
6 ounces hot Italian sausage, removed from the casing, if necessary
1 small yellow onion, diced
2 medium carrots, cut into 1-inch pieces
6 ounces cremini mushrooms, quartered
4 garlic cloves, minced
2 teaspoons sweet paprika
1 teaspoon garlic powder
1 teaspoon onion powder
1 teaspoon fennel seed, gently crushed
1 teaspoon red pepper flakes, plus more for serving
8 cups chicken stock
1 (14-ounce) can diced tomatoes, with their liquid
Kosher salt
1 bunch lacinato kale, leaves stemmed and chopped into 1-inch pieces
Freshly ground black pepper
1 (9-ounce) package prepared cheese tortellini
1 tablespoon red wine vinegar
Freshly grated Parmigiano-Reggiano cheese, for serving

In a large pot or Dutch oven, heat the olive oil over medium-high heat until it ripples. Add the sausage and cook, breaking it up into smaller pieces with a spoon, until well browned and cooked through, 4 to 6 minutes. Use a slotted spoon to transfer the sausage to a bowl, leaving all the fat behind in the pot.

Add the onion, carrots, and mushrooms to the pot. Cook, stirring occasionally, until the onion has begun to brown on the edges and the mushrooms have turned a deeper brown color, 5 to 7 minutes. Stir in the minced garlic, paprika, garlic powder, onion powder, fennel seed, and red pepper flakes. Cook to remove some of the raw garlic flavor and bloom the spices, 2 to 3 minutes more. Add the stock, tomatoes with their juices, and a generous pinch of salt.

Bring the soup to a boil over medium-high heat, then reduce the heat to medium-low and simmer, uncovered, to allow the flavors to meld, about 20 minutes. Once the carrots are tender all the way through, add the kale to the pot. Stir well to combine. Simmer until the kale is tender but not overcooked, 5 to 7 minutes more. Check the seasoning of the soup and adjust with salt and pepper.

Just before you're ready to serve, add the tortellini and cook for the time instructed on the package. As soon as the tortellini are finished, stir in the vinegar, then immediately ladle the soup into serving bowls and top with a pinch of red pepper flakes and a generous amount of freshly grated cheese.

Chicken and Buttermilk Dumpling Soup

WITH CRISPY CHICKEN SKIN

SERVES 4 TO 6

Chicken soup is undoubtedly one of the most comforting dishes around, but I sometimes find the texture to be too one-dimensional and it leaves me jonesing for a crunch to liven things up. I think I've found the solution here: crispy roasted chicken skin crumbled right on top! If you're one of those people who is weirded out by chicken skin, I promise this recipe will make you a believer. The dumpling batter is best mixed and cooked right away, so as tempting as it might be to get ahead in the recipe, make sure you only combine the wet and dry ingredients right before you're ready to scoop and cook them.

SOUP

2 tablespoons olive oil
6 bone-in or boneless, skin-on chicken thighs (1 to 1½ pounds total)
Kosher salt and freshly ground black pepper
2 medium carrots, cut into 1-inch pieces
3 celery stalks, cut into 1-inch pieces
1 small yellow onion, diced into 1-inch pieces
3 garlic cloves, finely chopped
6 cups chicken stock
6 to 8 thyme sprigs

DUMPLINGS

1½ cups all-purpose flour
1½ teaspoons kosher salt
1½ teaspoons chopped fresh thyme
1½ teaspoons chopped fresh dill, plus a few sprigs for garnish
1 teaspoon garlic powder
½ teaspoon baking powder
½ teaspoon baking soda
½ cup buttermilk
1 large egg yolk
1 tablespoon olive oil
Sour cream, for serving

Make the soup: Preheat the oven to 350°F. Line a small baking sheet with parchment paper or aluminum foil.

In a large pot or Dutch oven, heat the olive oil over medium-high heat until it ripples. Season the chicken thighs with salt and pepper, then place them skin-side down in the pan and cook until the skin is golden brown and crispy all over, 5 to 6 minutes. Flip the thighs and cook until slightly golden on the other side, 3 to 5 minutes more. Transfer to a plate to cool slightly, leaving all the fat behind in the pot.

Remove the skin from the thighs, leaving the thighs on the plate, and place the skins flat on the prepared baking sheet. Bake for 10 to 15 minutes, until the skins are crisp all the way through. Remove from the oven and let cool; they should snap like a cracker when fully cooled.

Meanwhile, to the pot with the chicken fat, add the carrots, celery, onion, and garlic. Cook over medium heat until the vegetables start to soften and have started to caramelize on the edges, 5 to 7 minutes.

Pour in the stock, then add the thyme and the seared chicken thighs. Bring to a simmer over medium-high heat, then reduce the heat to medium-low and simmer gently, uncovered, until the vegetables are tender and the chicken is fully cooked through and shreds easily, about 20 minutes. Use tongs or a slotted spoon to transfer the chicken thighs to a plate.

Recipe continues

Meanwhile, make the dumplings: In a large bowl, combine the flour, salt, thyme, dill, garlic powder, baking powder, and baking soda.

In a small bowl, whisk together the buttermilk, egg yolk, and olive oil. Right before you're ready to cook the dumplings, stir the egg mixture into the flour mixture to combine.

Use a cookie scoop or two spoons to form even, golf ball–size dumplings from the dough and drop them right into the simmering soup. (Dipping the spoon or scoop into the hot soup between portions will help give you a nice clean scoop.) You should end up with 12 to 16 dumplings total. Cover and cook over medium-low heat until the dumplings are cooked through, fluffy, and floating at the top of the soup, 10 to 15 minutes.

While the dumplings cook, shred the chicken thighs into bite-size pieces. Just before serving, return the shredded meat to the soup and stir to incorporate. Break up the crisp chicken skins into ½- to 1-inch pieces.

Ladle the soup into bowls, then top each serving with a dollop of sour cream, a sprinkle of the crispy chicken skin, and a few fresh dill sprigs. Serve immediately.

Corn and Poblano Chowder

WITH CHILI TORTILLA CRISPS

SERVES 4

This dish is full of bright, summery flavors condensed into a warm, comforting soup that was perfect for my eight years of foggy San Francisco summer days—and still is perfect for a true winter day in need of some levity. The secret is the corn-infused stock you make with corn cobs and scrapings. Gently simmering them into the broth and milk gives you a flavorful, slightly sweetened base that ensures the corn is the star of the show and amps up the subtle spice from the poblano peppers. Don't skimp on the shattered tortilla crisps!

SOUP

2 ears sweet corn, shucked
4 cups chicken stock or vegetable stock, plus more as needed
2 cups whole milk, plus more as needed
2 slices thick-cut bacon, cut into ½-inch pieces
2 tablespoons butter
1 small yellow onion, diced into ¼-inch pieces
2 poblano peppers, seeded and diced into ¼-inch pieces
3 or 4 garlic cloves, minced
3 tablespoons all-purpose flour
1 (4-ounce) can diced green chiles (I like Hatch chiles!), with their liquid
1 teaspoon garlic powder
1 teaspoon onion powder
1 teaspoon ground cumin
Kosher salt and freshly ground black pepper
¼ cup chopped fresh cilantro, plus more leaves for serving

TORTILLA CRISPS

4 (8-inch) corn tortillas, cut into quarters
1 to 2 tablespoons olive oil
2 teaspoons chili powder
Kosher salt

Make the soup: Cut the kernels off the corncobs and set the kernels aside in a small bowl. Working one at a time, hold each cob upright inside a medium pot and, using the back of a knife or a butter knife, scrape any remaining corn off the cobs directly into the pot. Cut or snap the cobs in half and add them to the pot along with the stock and the milk. Bring to a simmer over medium heat, then reduce the heat to low, cover, and cook for at least 20 minutes, or up to 45 minutes, to infuse the stock and milk with all that lovely corn flavor.

Meanwhile, place the bacon and butter in a separate large pot or Dutch oven. Cook over medium heat, stirring frequently, just until the bacon strips are a deep, rich brown and crispy, 5 to 7 minutes. Transfer the bacon to a plate, leaving the rendered fat in the pot.

Add the onion and poblanos to the pot with the bacon fat and cook over medium heat, stirring frequently, just until the edges of the onion have taken on a bit of color and the peppers have softened, 5 to 7 minutes. Add the garlic and cook for 1 minute more, then sprinkle the flour over the vegetables. Stir well to combine and cook until the raw flour taste has cooked out, 2 to 3 minutes.

Using tongs, carefully remove the corncobs from the stock and discard them. Pour the stock into the pot with the onion and poblano, then immediately stir well to break up any lumps of flour that may have formed.

Add the reserved corn kernels, the chiles and their liquid, garlic powder, onion powder, and cumin to the pot. Stir to combine, then taste and adjust the seasoning with salt and

Recipe and ingredients continue

FOR SERVING (OPTIONAL)

Diced ripe Hass avocado
Sour cream
1 or 2 limes, cut into wedges
Sliced radishes
Sliced jalapeños
Crumbled Cotija cheese

black pepper. Reduce the heat to medium-low and cook uncovered, stirring occasionally, until the soup has the consistency of buttermilk or thin yogurt (think classic clam chowder!), about 30 minutes. If it's too thick, add a touch more milk or stock.

Meanwhile, make the tortilla crisps: Preheat the oven to 350°F. Line a baking sheet with parchment paper or aluminum foil.

Arrange the tortilla quarters on the prepared baking sheet and drizzle with the olive oil. Sprinkle with the chili powder and some salt, then massage the seasonings and oil into each tortilla quarter. Bake for 10 to 12 minutes, until the tortilla chips are crisp all the way through and a deep, rich golden color.

Just before serving the soup, stir in the cilantro and crispy bacon, then taste and adjust the seasoning as needed. Ladle the soup into bowls, then shatter a few of the tortilla crisps on top of each bowl. Garnish with a few cilantro leaves if desired, and add some diced avocado, a dollop of sour cream, a squeeze of fresh lime juice, or any other toppings you want!

Garlicky Bread Soup

SERVES 4 TO 6

I bake two to four loaves of sourdough bread a week, and on the rare occasion there is any left over, this is my go-to recipe. The gentle bitterness from the escarole and bright finish of the red wine vinegar are the key to keeping this one from feeling too heavy. VEG

2 tablespoons olive oil
1 small yellow onion, diced into 1-inch pieces
6 garlic cloves, very thinly sliced
6 cups vegetable stock
1 (15-ounce) can chickpeas, drained and rinsed
2 teaspoons granulated garlic
1 teaspoon red pepper flakes
10 to 12 ounces day-old sourdough bread or baguette, cut or torn into 2-inch pieces (3 to 4 heaping cups)
1 head escarole, cut into 1- to 2-inch pieces
2 tablespoons red wine vinegar
Kosher salt and freshly ground black pepper
Shaved Pecorino Romano cheese, for serving

In a large pot or Dutch oven, heat the olive oil over medium heat until it ripples. Add the onion and cook just until translucent and barely taking on some color on the edges, 5 to 7 minutes. Stir in the sliced garlic and cook until fragrant, 1 to 2 minutes more.

Add the stock, chickpeas, granulated garlic, and red pepper flakes to the pot and stir to combine. Simmer to give the flavors a chance to meld, about 15 minutes.

Just before serving, add the bread pieces and the escarole to the soup and stir well to combine. Simmer until the bread softens and starts to break down slightly, thickening the soup, 5 to 7 minutes. (You want the bread to soak up the broth and become soft, but not totally fall apart and turn to mush.) Stir in the vinegar, a hefty pinch or two of salt, and some pepper.

Ladle the soup into bowls, garnish with the cheese, and serve hot.

STAUB

PASTA

Melted Sungold and Saffron Orecchiette

SERVES 4 TO 6

The ultimate summer pasta, this dish is best made when Sungold cherry tomatoes are at their peak. Their beautiful golden color melds perfectly with the subtlety of the saffron, and provides an unexpected flavor profile in what might look like a simple tomato sauce. You can easily sub the Sungolds out for red cherry tomatoes. The resulting dish will be more red-orange than the striking yellow-gold, but no less delicious. VEG

2 pints Sungold cherry tomatoes
¼ cup plus 1 tablespoon olive oil
¼ cup thinly sliced fresh basil leaves, plus some torn leaves for serving
2 tablespoons white balsamic vinegar (dark balsamic works, too)
Small pinch of red pepper flakes, plus more for serving
Kosher salt
2 small shallots, thinly sliced into rings
3 or 4 garlic cloves, minced
1 teaspoon ground turmeric
1 teaspoon garlic powder
1 teaspoon sweet paprika
Small pinch of saffron (about ⅛ teaspoon)
2 cups vegetable stock
1 pound dry orecchiette pasta
4 tablespoons (½ stick) butter, cut into 4 pieces
Freshly ground black pepper
Shaved Parmigiano-Reggiano cheese, for serving

Cut 1 pint of the tomatoes in half, then place in a medium bowl. Add 1 tablespoon of the olive oil, the basil, vinegar, red pepper flakes, and a generous pinch of salt. Mix well and let marinate at room temperature.

In a medium pot or Dutch oven, heat the remaining ¼ cup olive oil over medium heat until it begins to ripple. Add the shallots and cook, stirring frequently, just until the shallots begin to brown, about 2 minutes. Add the remaining 1 pint tomatoes and cook, stirring occasionally, until the tomatoes have begun to burst, 3 to 5 minutes. Add the garlic and cook for 2 to 3 minutes more until slightly browned.

Reduce the heat to medium-low. Add the turmeric, garlic powder, paprika, saffron, and a big pinch of salt and stir well. Cook for 30 to 60 seconds until fragrant and lightly toasted, then carefully pour in the stock. Reduce the heat to low, cover, and simmer, stirring now and then, for 20 to 25 minutes until the tomatoes have cooked down and the shallots are very soft.

Meanwhile, bring a large pot of salted water to a boil over high heat. Add the orecchiette and cook according to the package directions until al dente. Reserve 1 cup of the pasta cooking water, then drain.

Meanwhile, carefully transfer the tomato sauce to a blender and add the butter. Start blending on low, then slowly increase to high and blend until you have a smooth sauce, about 1 minute. Taste and adjust the seasoning as needed, then return the sauce to the pot over medium-low heat.

Add the orecchiette to the sauce and stir well. Add a bit of the reserved pasta water as needed to adjust the consistency. Cook until the pasta has absorbed the sauce nicely and each noodle is evenly coated, 1 to 2 minutes.

Just before serving, scatter the marinated tomatoes over the pasta and top with freshly shaved Parmigiano, torn basil leaves, and red pepper flakes.

DBG (Death by Garlic) Rotini

SERVES 4 TO 6

A hyper-garlicky, vegetarian twist on the carbonara technique we all love so much, this dish gives you varied and layered garlic flavor. The cloves are prepared two ways—roasted for sweetness and depth and toasted for texture and a stronger bite of allium, with a bright finish from the freshly chopped chives. This is best eaten as soon as it's mixed up, so make sure you work quickly! VEG

1 head garlic, kept whole, plus 6 to 8 garlic cloves, minced
¼ cup plus 1 tablespoon olive oil
Kosher salt
¾ cup freshly grated Pecorino Romano cheese, plus more shaved for garnish
4 large eggs
2 large egg yolks
¼ cup thinly sliced fresh chives
2 teaspoons freshly ground black pepper
1 teaspoon granulated garlic or garlic powder
1 pound dry rotini pasta
Red pepper flakes, for garnish

Preheat the oven to 325°F.

Cut the garlic head in half crosswise, then drizzle the cut sides with 1 tablespoon of the olive oil and sprinkle with a hefty pinch of salt. Tightly wrap each half in a piece of aluminum foil and place them on a baking sheet. Bake for 45 minutes, then carefully unwrap one half to check for doneness. You want the garlic to be a rich taupe color, slightly caramelized on the tops, and completely soft; if it's not quite there yet, bake for 10 to 15 minutes more. Let the garlic cool completely, about 30 minutes.

In a small sauté pan, heat the remaining ¼ cup olive oil over medium heat. Add the minced garlic and stir well. Cook, stirring frequently, until it has barely begun to turn a light golden brown color, 2 to 3 minutes, then immediately remove from the heat. Let cool.

Bring a large pot of heavily salted water to a boil over high heat.

Meanwhile, in a large bowl, combine the cheese, eggs, egg yolks, chives, black pepper, granulated garlic, and a heavy pinch of salt. Squeeze the roasted garlic cloves from their skins into the bowl, then whisk well to combine, ensuring all the roasted garlic is broken up and the mixture is smooth. Whisk in the garlic-oil mixture.

Add the pasta to the boiling water and cook according to the package directions until al dente. Reserve 2 cups of the pasta cooking water, then drain the pasta and immediately add it to the egg mixture. Quickly add ½ cup of the reserved cooking water and stir briskly to combine and coat all the noodles. The pasta should be glossy and each noodle should be well coated, but not swimming in liquid. As needed, add another ¼ to ½ cup pasta water and stir well.

Dish up the pasta immediately and garnish with a bit of shaved cheese and a pinch of red pepper flakes.

Cauliflower Brown Butter Pasta

WITH GARLICKY CROUTONS

SERVES 4 TO 6

Yes, this pasta is delicious by itself, but the super crunchy, garlicky chunks of bread lift it to another level. This dish works so well because of the balance of its ingredients; nutty brown butter and warm cauliflower play well together, while Pecorino's bite and a little zip of lemon ties everything together for your secret-weapon cozy weeknight dinner. Pair with some simple grilled chicken for a more substantial supper, or if you're feeding a larger group. VEG

GARLICKY CROUTONS

2 tablespoons olive oil
1 cup ¼-inch cubes day-old bread, or 1 cup panko breadcrumbs
4 garlic cloves, minced
Kosher salt and freshly ground black pepper
1 tablespoon finely chopped fresh parsley, plus more for garnish

PASTA

Kosher salt
1 pound dry mezze rigatoni or other pasta shape of your choice
6 tablespoons (¾ stick) butter
1 small head cauliflower (about 1 pound), cut into small florets
1 large shallot, sliced into rings
½ cup freshly grated Pecorino Romano cheese
Zest and juice of ½ lemon
Freshly ground black pepper

Make the croutons: In a small skillet, heat the olive oil over medium heat until it ripples. Add the bread and stir well to coat with the oil. Cook until the bread starts to turn a very light golden color, then add the garlic and season with salt and pepper. (If you're using panko instead of bread, add the panko and garlic to the pan at the same time, as panko will toast more quickly.) Cook until the bread is toasted and crispy and the garlic is slightly brown, 3 to 4 minutes, then remove from the heat and let cool. Sprinkle with the parsley.

Make the pasta: Bring a large pot of salted water to a boil over high heat. Add the pasta and cook for 1 to 2 minutes less than the package directions for al dente. Reserve 1 cup of the pasta cooking water, then drain.

Meanwhile, heat a large saucepan over medium-high heat for about 1 minute. When the pan is ripping hot and smoking a bit, add 4 tablespoons of the butter and swirl the pan as it melts. Cook until the butter smells nutty and takes on some color, then reduce the heat to low and add the cauliflower and shallot. Cook, stirring frequently, until the edges of the cauliflower and shallot are browning, 4 to 6 minutes. Add the pasta and reserved cooking water, increase the heat to medium, and cook until the pasta looks glossy and most of the liquid has evaporated, 3 to 5 minutes. Add the cheese, lemon zest, lemon juice, and remaining 2 tablespoons butter, then season with salt and pepper. Stir well to coat, then taste and adjust the seasoning one last time as needed, before transferring to a serving bowl.

Top the pasta with the croutons and a bit more parsley, and serve immediately.

Red Wine Lamb Meatballs

WITH SPAGHETTI

SERVES 4 TO 6

These lamb meatballs are next-level thanks to the red wine reduction folded into the mixture. It's an unexpected step that renders the meatballs super flavorful and moist. In this recipe, we bake the meatballs as opposed to browning them in the pan and, yes, I am fully aware of how controversial that is. It's quicker and cleaner, and it gives you time to start the sauce as they cook in the oven, which helps make this a practical weeknight dinner instead of a massive project. But, if you can hear your nonna shaming you in your head, go ahead and brown them in the Dutch oven you plan to make the sauce in.

MEATBALLS

2 tablespoons olive oil, plus more for greasing
1 cup red wine (I like cabernet or merlot)
¼ medium yellow onion, finely diced (about ⅓ cup)
2 garlic cloves, finely chopped
¼ cup panko or Italian breadcrumbs
2 tablespoons whole milk
1 pound ground lamb
8 ounces hot or mild Italian sausage, removed from the casing if necessary
¼ cup freshly grated Parmigiano-Reggiano cheese
1 large egg
1 large egg yolk
2 teaspoons kosher salt
1 teaspoon dried basil
1 teaspoon sweet paprika
1 teaspoon red pepper flakes
1 teaspoon garlic powder
1 tablespoon chopped fresh basil

Make the meatballs: Preheat the oven to 425°F. Line a baking sheet with aluminum foil and grease it with olive oil.

In a small pot, bring the wine to a low (not rolling) boil over medium heat. Cook at a low boil, swirling the pot occasionally, until it reaches a syrupy consistency and has reduced to ¼ cup, 15 to 20 minutes. (Avoid the temptation to turn up the heat, as it can scorch.) Remove from the heat and let cool completely, 15 to 20 minutes.

In a small sauté pan, heat the olive oil over medium heat until it ripples. Add the onion and cook until it just begins to take on a bit of color, 2 to 3 minutes, then add the garlic and cook, stirring frequently, until the mixture is slightly brown and very fragrant, and the onions have softened slightly, 2 to 3 minutes more. Remove from the heat and let cool a bit.

In a large bowl, mix together the breadcrumbs and milk and let stand for a minute or two to hydrate. Add the onion mixture, lamb, sausage, cheese, egg, egg yolk, salt, dried basil, paprika, red pepper flakes, and garlic powder. Add the wine mixture and fresh basil and use your hands or a wooden spoon to thoroughly combine. (At this point, I like to cook off a small piece and taste-test it to check the seasoning.)

Form the meat mixture into 12 to 16 meatballs and place them on the prepared baking sheet. Bake for about 12 minutes, until they begin to brown nicely and start to release some liquid.

Meanwhile, make the sauce: In a large Dutch oven, heat the olive oil over medium-high heat until it ripples. Add the onion and cook, stirring frequently, until it starts to take on nice brown color on the edges, 3 to

Recipe and ingredients continue

SAUCE

¼ cup olive oil
¾ medium yellow onion, diced
2 garlic cloves, chopped
1 cup red wine
2 (14-ounce) cans diced tomatoes, with their juices
1 (14-ounce) can tomato puree
2 tablespoons chopped fresh basil
2 teaspoons garlic powder
2 teaspoons onion powder
2 teaspoons dried basil
Pinch of red pepper flakes
1 Parmigiano-Reggiano cheese rind (optional)
Kosher salt

FOR SERVING

Kosher salt
8 to 10 ounces dry spaghetti
Torn fresh basil
Grated Parmigiano-Reggiano cheese

4 minutes. Add the garlic and cook for another minute or two. Carefully add the wine and stir with a wooden spoon, scraping up any browned bits from the bottom of the pot. Cook until the wine has reduced by about half, 8 to 10 minutes, then reduce the heat to medium-low and add the diced tomatoes and their juices, the tomato puree, fresh basil, garlic powder, onion powder, dried basil, red pepper flakes, and cheese rind (if using). Stir well and season with a bit of salt. Cook, stirring occasionally, until very aromatic and the sauce has turned a slightly richer red color, 15 to 20 minutes.

Add the meatballs to the sauce, along with any liquid on the baking sheet. Stir well to coat the meatballs with the sauce, then cover and simmer, stirring every 5 to 10 minutes, for 45 minutes to 1 hour. After about 30 minutes, taste and adjust the seasoning as needed. You'll know the sauce is done when the flavor has gone from bright, acidic, and tomatoey to more luscious, rich, and umami-forward.

Meanwhile, bring a large pot of salted water to a boil over high heat. Add the spaghetti and cook according to the package directions until al dente, then drain.

Plate the pasta in shallow individual bowls or on a large shallow serving platter. Right before serving, stir some fresh basil into the sauce. Ladle the meatballs and sauce over the cooked pasta and garnish with a smattering of freshly grated cheese.

Sweet Potato "Gnocchi"

WITH HAZELNUT GREMOLATA AND BARELY WILTED ARUGULA

SERVES 4 TO 6

Gnocchi are notoriously difficult to conquer, but fear not, this recipe uses sweet potato starch in lieu of traditional flour for a more foolproof version with a delightfully mochi-like texture! Sweet potato starch has no gluten, so you don't risk overworking the dough and ending up with dense gnocchi. The key to good gnocchi is *juuust* enough starch to bind the dough and make it manageable, without adding so much it becomes tough and dry. Go slow and let your instincts lead—once the dough has formed, holds its shape, and is reminiscent of Play-Doh, you know you're there. Even if you don't plan on eating all the gnocchi, I recommend cooking them all and freezing any leftovers—just cool, toss in a bit of olive oil, transfer to a zip-top bag, and freeze. Thaw in the fridge overnight before reheating. **VEG, GF**

GNOCCHI

- 2 medium sweet potatoes (about 1½ pounds)
- 1 large egg
- Kosher salt
- 1½ to 2 cups sweet potato starch or white potato starch

HAZELNUT GREMOLATA

- ½ cup chopped hazelnuts, toasted
- ¼ cup olive oil
- ¼ cup finely chopped fresh parsley
- 2 or 3 garlic cloves, grated or minced
- 1 tablespoon finely chopped fresh sage
- Zest and juice of 1 lemon
- Kosher salt and freshly ground black pepper

Make the gnocchi: Use a fork or small knife to prick the sweet potatoes a few times all over. Microwave the sweet potatoes for 8 to 10 minutes, until they are completely soft. Place them in a large bowl, cover with plastic wrap, and let stand for 5 to 10 minutes. (Alternatively, bake them at 400°F for 45 to 60 minutes, until tender.)

Peel the cooled sweet potatoes, then place the cooked flesh in a large bowl and mash with a fork or pass through a potato ricer. Add the egg and a large pinch of salt and mix well. Add 1 cup of the sweet potato starch and mix well with a fork to combine, then mix with your hands as the dough comes together. It should be slightly sticky but should hold its shape well; continue adding the starch ¼ cup at a time as needed until you have a smooth, workable dough. Wrap the dough in plastic wrap and refrigerate for 30 minutes or up to overnight.

Meanwhile, make the gremolata: In a small bowl, combine the hazelnuts, olive oil, parsley, garlic, sage, lemon zest, lemon juice, and plenty of salt and pepper. Stir well to combine, then cover and refrigerate.

Cook the gnocchi: Bring a large pot of salted water to a boil over high heat. Fill a large bowl with ice and

Recipe and ingredients continue

FOR SERVING

4 tablespoons (½ stick) butter
2 large handfuls of baby arugula (2 to 3 cups)
Kosher salt and freshly ground black pepper
½ cup shaved Pecorino Romano cheese

water. Line a plate with paper towels and place it near the ice bath.

Pinch off a small amount (about 2 teaspoons) of the dough and roll it into a perfect sphere with your hands, then carefully drop it into the boiling water. (You can also use a ½-ounce cookie scoop for more consistently shaped gnocchi!) Repeat until you've added one-quarter to one-third of the dough to the water. Cook until the gnocchi float to the surface, 2 to 3 minutes, then cook until cooked through in the center, 2 minutes more. Using a slotted spoon, transfer the gnocchi to the ice bath to quickly stop the cooking. Allow to cool completely in the ice bath, about 1 to 2 minutes, before moving them to the paper towel–lined plate to dry. Repeat the cooking and cooling process with the remaining dough.

In a large cast-iron skillet or sauté pan, melt the butter over medium-high heat. Add the gnocchi and stir to coat. Cook, undisturbed, until they've started to brown on the bottom, 2 to 3 minutes, then stir to flip them. Cook until brown on another side, 2 to 3 minutes more. Remove from the heat and add the arugula. Stir so the arugula barely begins to wilt, then season everything with salt and pepper.

Divide the gnocchi among individual serving bowls, then dot the top of each bowl with a few spoonfuls of the gremolata. Sprinkle some shaved cheese over the top and dig in!

Chorizo and Clam Linguine

SERVES 4 TO 6

My first introduction to the combination of pork and seafood was during culinary school, when our chef made a juicy grilled pork chop lathered in a creamy chorizo and clam sauce—it was a revelation. Luxurious but light, sophisticated but homey. This recipe is an homage to that dish. It's the linguine and clams we all wish we got when we ate out but never knew we were missing!

Kosher salt
1 pound dry linguine
¼ cup olive oil
2 small shallots, thinly sliced into rings
4 garlic cloves, chopped
4 ounces dry Spanish chorizo, sliced into ¼-inch thick half moons
2½ pounds fresh clams, such as littlenecks, scrubbed well
1 cup dry white wine
1 (6½-ounce) can chopped clams, drained, liquid reserved
4 tablespoons (½ stick) butter
¼ cup chopped fresh parsley
Zest and juice of 1 lemon
Toasted crusty bread, for serving (optional)

Bring a large pot of salted water to a boil over high heat. Add the linguine and cook for 1 to 2 minutes shy of the package directions for al dente. Reserve 1 cup of the pasta cooking water, then drain the linguine.

Meanwhile, in a large skillet, heat the olive oil over medium heat until it ripples. Toss in the shallots and cook, stirring frequently, for about 1 minute, until the shallots have started to turn translucent, then add the garlic and cook until softened, lightly browned, and fragrant, 2 to 3 minutes.

Add the chorizo to the skillet and cook until it starts to release its oils and becomes super fragrant, another 2 to 3 minutes, then add the fresh clams. Pour in the wine and cover the pan to trap in all the steam. Cook just until the clams have popped open, 8 to 10 minutes. Discard any clams that do not open.

Add the cooked linguine to the clam-chorizo mixture, then add the canned clams and their liquid. Toss to coat the linguine evenly with the sauce and cook over medium heat so the pasta absorbs the liquid and finishes cooking, 1 to 2 minutes, stirring frequently. If the pasta soaks up too much sauce, add some of the reserved cooking water to loosen it. The dish is finished when the liquid looks glossy and nicely coats all the linguine noodles—it should not be watery.

Just before serving, stir in the butter, the parsley, lemon zest, and lemon juice. Serve with lots of toasted crusty bread alongside.

CHENIN

STAUB

Rainbow Chard Pasta Rolls

WITH BLUSHING TOMATO SAUCE

MAKES 12 ROLLS

Since we're feeling *a little bit extra*, we might as well gussy up a lasagna! This dish has all the comforting elements of the classic, only we're putting in the effort to make individual portions. Each lasagna sheet has plenty of filling and is doused in a creamy tomato sauce and finished in the broiler for a luxurious, melty twist on a comfy classic. The lemon juice and zest offset the richness of the creamy tomato sauce and mozzarella to make this a crushable dish. **VEG**

SAUCE

¼ cup olive oil
6 garlic cloves, minced
¼ cup tomato paste
1 teaspoon sweet paprika
1 (14-ounce) can tomato puree (or sauce)
1 cup heavy cream
2 tablespoons finely chopped fresh basil

ROLLS

Kosher salt
12 dry lasagna noodles
2 tablespoons olive oil, plus more for the noodles
½ medium yellow onion, diced into ¼-inch pieces
1 bunch rainbow chard, leaves stemmed and chopped into 1-inch pieces
16 ounces whole-milk ricotta cheese, homemade (see page 154) or store-bought
8 ounces shredded low-moisture mozzarella cheese
½ cup shaved Parmigiano-Reggiano cheese, plus more for serving
¼ cup Italian breadcrumbs
1 large egg
Zest and juice of 1 small lemon
Freshly ground black pepper
1 (16-ounce) log fresh mozzarella cheese
Fresh basil leaves, for serving

Make the sauce: In a large skillet, combine the olive oil and garlic. Cook over medium heat, stirring frequently, until the garlic is fragrant and starts to take on a bit of brown color, 1 to 2 minutes. Quickly stir in the tomato paste and paprika and cook for 1 to 2 minutes to bloom the paprika. Gently pour in the tomato puree and cream and whisk well. Add ½ cup water to the tomato puree can or box, swish it around, and pour it into the pot with the sauce. Bring to a simmer and cook for about 5 minutes, then reduce the heat to low, cover, and let it hang out while you assemble the rolls.

Make the rolls: Bring a large pot of heavily salted water to a boil over high heat. Add the lasagna noodles and cook for a minute or two shy of the package directions for al dente (the pasta will cook more in the sauce). Drain, then run cold water over the noodles until they're fully cooled. Toss them with a bit of olive oil to prevent sticking.

In a large sauté pan, heat the olive oil over medium-high heat until it ripples. Add the onion and cook until slightly translucent and the edges have barely begun to brown, 2 to 3 minutes. Add the chard and cook just until wilted, about 1 minute. Remove from the heat and let cool slightly in the pan, then transfer to a large bowl. Add the ricotta, shredded mozzarella, Parmigiano, breadcrumbs, egg, lemon zest, and lemon juice. Season with salt and pepper and mix well to combine.

Slice 12 thin slices (about ⅛ inch thick) from the log of fresh mozzarella. Chop the remaining mozzarella into small cubes and fold them into the Swiss chard mixture.

Preheat the oven to 375°F.

Recipe continues

Stir the chopped basil into the tomato sauce, then pour about half the sauce into a 9 × 13-inch baking dish and spread it evenly over the bottom.

Lay the noodles out on a clean countertop or baking sheet—I like to do 4 to 6 at a time. Place about ¼ cup of the chard-ricotta mixture onto each noodle and use a small spoon or knife to spread it evenly from one end to the other. Roll up each noodle tightly to enclose the filling, then place the rolls seam-side down in the sauce in the baking dish. Repeat with the remaining noodles and filling.

Evenly distribute the remaining sauce over each roll, then cover the baking dish tightly with aluminum foil. Bake for 25 to 30 minutes, until the sauce is bubbling and the rolls are heated through. Remove the pan from the oven and switch the oven to broil on high. Remove the foil and place one slice of mozzarella on top of each roll. Broil for 2 to 3 minutes, just until the cheese is melty, bubbling, and golden. Keep a close eye on the rolls to avoid burning.

Serve garnished with basil and more shaved Parmigiano.

Two-Pork Beer Ragù

WITH PAPPARDELLE

SERVES 4 TO 6

If you're looking for the perfect slow Sunday supper recipe, you've found it. The combo of smoky bacon and fall-apart braised pork shoulder makes the perfect topping for some lightly buttered pappardelle noodles, and the vinegar is a bright finish to cut some of the richness. While this dish may take some time to cook, it is by no means time *consuming*. Once the ragù is in the oven, you have plenty of time to lounge about while your home fills with the aroma of stewing tomatoes and herbs—a sure antidote to even the worst case of Sunday Scaries.

1 tablespoon olive oil
4 slices thick-cut bacon, cut into 1-inch pieces
1½ to 2 pounds boneless pork shoulder, cut into 2-inch cubes
Kosher salt and freshly ground black pepper
1 medium yellow onion, diced into ½-inch pieces
2 small carrots, cut into 1-inch pieces
6 garlic cloves, thinly sliced
3 tablespoons tomato paste
12 ounces light beer, such as lager or Belgian wheat
1 tablespoon chopped fresh thyme
1 tablespoon chopped fresh sage
1 teaspoon garlic powder
1 teaspoon onion powder
Pinch of red pepper flakes
1 (28-ounce) can whole peeled tomatoes, with their juices
1 Parmigiano-Reggiano cheese rind (optional)
1 tablespoon red wine vinegar or balsamic vinegar

Make your own pappardelle—instructions are on the next page!

Preheat the oven to 325°F.

Place the olive oil and bacon in a large Dutch oven. Cook over medium heat, stirring frequently, until the bacon is browned and crisp about halfway through, 2 to 3 minutes. Transfer the bacon to a large plate, reserving the rendered fat in the pot.

Season the pork shoulder with salt and black pepper, then, working in batches as needed to avoid overcrowding, add it to the Dutch oven. Cook the pork over medium-high heat until light golden brown on all sides, 3 to 4 minutes per side. Transfer the pork to the plate with the bacon.

Reduce the heat to medium, then add the onion and carrots to the pot and cook until the edges of the onion have started to brown slightly, about 3 minutes. Add the garlic and cook until lightly brown, about 2 minutes more. Add the tomato paste and use your spoon to work it into the veggies and spread it evenly all over the bottom of the pot. Cook for 2 to 3 minutes, until the veggies and the bottom of the Dutch oven are well coated and the tomato paste is very fragrant, then add the beer and stir well, scraping up all the browned bits from the bottom of the pot and breaking up all the tomato paste.

Add the thyme, sage, garlic powder, onion powder, red pepper flakes, a big pinch of salt, and some black pepper. Cook until the mixture has reduced by half, 5 to 7 minutes, then add the tomatoes and their juices, crushing the tomatoes with your hands as you drop them into the pot. Stir in the cheese rind (if using), then return the seared pork and bacon to the pot and stir to combine.

Recipe and ingredients continue

8 to 12 ounces pappardelle pasta, homemade (recipe follows) or store-bought
2 tablespoons butter
2 tablespoons chopped fresh parsley
Freshly grated Parmigiano-Reggiano cheese, for serving

Cover the Dutch oven and pop it into the oven. Cook for 2 to 2½ hours, stirring every 30 minutes, until the pork is super tender and starts to fall apart if you stir the ragù. Uncover the pot, stir in the vinegar, cover again, and turn the oven off. Let the ragù hang out in the warm oven while you cook the pasta.

Bring a large pot of salted water to a boil over high heat. Add the pappardelle and cook according to the package directions until al dente, then drain. Transfer the pasta to a large bowl, then throw in the butter, parsley, and a good pinch each of salt and black pepper. Toss well to coat.

Divvy up the noodles among individual bowls, top each with the hot ragù and some freshly grated cheese, and enjoy with an ice-cold beer! Let any leftover ragù cool, then transfer it to a zip-top bag or airtight container in the fridge for up to a week or in the freezer for up to a month.

Fresh Pappardelle Pasta

MAKES 8 TO 12 OUNCES

2 large eggs
6 large egg yolks
2 tablespoons olive oil
3 scant cups all-purpose or 00 flour, plus more as needed
2 teaspoons kosher salt

In a medium bowl, whisk together the eggs, egg yolks, and olive oil. Place the flour and salt in a food processor. With the motor running, drizzle in the egg mixture and process until the dough has formed into a shaggy mass, 30 to 45 seconds.

Turn the dough out onto a work surface and knead for 3 to 4 minutes. The dough should be firm, but fairly easy to work with. If it's too wet, knead in 1 to 2 tablespoons more flour.

Cover the pasta dough with plastic wrap and let it rest in the fridge for at least 1 hour or up to overnight. You can now cut the dough into 4 even portions and use a pasta machine or rolling pin to roll each portion into sheets of your desired thickness. Cut the sheets into roughly 1-foot-long sections, then cut them lengthwise into 1-inch-wide noodles. Cook in heavily salted boiling water for about 2 minutes (yes, that fast!) before draining and serving with the ragù.

Lemony Ricotta Gnudi

WITH MAITAKE MUSHROOMS AND SHRIMP

SERVES 4 TO 6

Gnocchi are tricky to master (see page 111), so consider these ricotta gnudi as a beginner's intro to the world of dumpling-style pasta. Here, we swap cooked potato for creamy ricotta cheese. The dough comes together fairly easily, but take care not to overwork it. The gnudi will become tough and gummy if you overmix , as it will cause too much gluten to develop.

---

16 ounces whole-milk ricotta cheese
2 large eggs
½ cup finely grated Parmigiano-Reggiano cheese
Zest of 2 lemons
1 tablespoon chopped fresh dill, plus a small handful of dill sprigs (about ¼ cup) for garnish
2 teaspoons kosher salt, plus more as needed
1 teaspoon garlic powder
Freshly ground black pepper
1 cup 00 or semolina flour, plus more for dusting
4 tablespoons (½ stick) butter
8 ounces maitake mushrooms, cleaned and separated into bite-size wedges
1 small shallot, sliced into rings
1 pound shrimp (16 to 20 count), peeled and deveined
Juice of 1 lemon
Small pinch of red pepper flakes

In a large bowl, whisk or stir together the ricotta, eggs, Parmigiano, zest of 1 lemon, chopped dill, salt, garlic powder, and some black pepper to combine. Add the flour and mix gently with a spoon just until the flour is incorporated and a soft dough forms.

Bring a large pot of heavily salted water to a gentle boil over medium-high heat. Fill a large bowl with ice and water and set it near the stove. Line a plate with paper towels and place it near the ice bath.

Lightly dust a baking sheet with flour. Using lightly floured hands, shape the dough into small balls, about 1 inch in diameter—you should have 30 to 35 balls. (I find a small cookie scoop works well to keep them consistent in shape and size.) Place them on the prepared baking sheet. Working in batches of 10 to 12 at a time, carefully drop the ricotta balls into the boiling water and cook until they float to the surface, 3 to 4 minutes. Using a slotted spoon or strainer, transfer the cooked gnudi to the ice bath to cool for a minute or two, then transfer them to the paper towel–lined plate to drain. Repeat with the remaining gnudi. Reserve ½ cup of the cooking water and discard the rest.

In a large sauté or cast-iron pan, melt 2 tablespoons of the butter over medium heat. Add the mushrooms and shallot and cook until the mushrooms have softened a bit and the shallot has just begun to brown on the edges, 4 to 5 minutes. Add the shrimp and cook until they have begun to turn pink but aren't quite cooked through, 2 to 3 minutes per side. Season with salt and black pepper, then add all the gnudi along with the reserved cooking water. Cook until the water has begun to thicken and coat everything well and the shrimp are cooked through, 3 to 4 minutes. Add the zest of the remaining lemon, the lemon juice, and red pepper flakes to the pan and toss to coat everything evenly. Remove from the heat and stir in the remaining 2 tablespoons butter.

To serve, arrange the gnudi on individual plates or a large platter, then spoon the shrimp mixture over the top. Garnish with fresh dill sprigs just before digging in!

RICE, BEANS & GRAINS

Tomatillo Arroz Verde

SERVES 4 TO 6

I love classic red Spanish rice like no other—it was a staple growing up we had at least twice a week with dinner. This rice calls into play the same technique of blending aromatics to create a deeply flavorful cooking liquid, then toasting the rice to give it a nice round nuttiness once it's cooked. Tomatillos replace the traditional tomatoes here and give the rice a refreshingly tart finish that makes it a perfect complement to so many dishes—my favorite being the Achiote-Marinated Shrimp and Pineapple Skewers (page 204). Look for golf ball–size tomatillos or smaller. GF

---

6 small tomatillos, husked and rinsed well
¼ cup tightly packed fresh cilantro, plus 1 tablespoon chopped cilantro
Kosher salt
Juice of 1 lime
3 tablespoons olive oil
2 teaspoons chicken bouillon powder, or 1 bouillon cube (optional, but recommended)
1 teaspoon ground cumin
½ teaspoon dried Mexican oregano
½ small white onion, diced into ¼-inch pieces
1½ cups uncooked long-grain white rice
2 garlic cloves, minced
2 tablespoons butter

Cut 3 of the tomatillos into roughly ¼-inch cubes, then place them in a small bowl. Sprinkle with the chopped cilantro and a good pinch of salt, then add half of the lime juice and 1 tablespoon of the olive oil. Mix well and set aside to marinate.

In a blender, combine the remaining 3 tomatillos, the remaining ¼ cup cilantro, bouillon (if using), the oregano, cumin, a hefty pinch of salt, and 3 cups water. Blend on high speed until the tomatillos are completely pureed, about 1 minute.

In a large pan with a lid, heat the remaining 2 tablespoons olive oil over medium heat until it ripples. Add the onion and cook, stirring frequently, until it begins to turn translucent, about 2 minutes, then add the rice and garlic. Stir well and cook for about 4 minutes to toast the rice mixture and give it a nice rich flavor; it's done when the garlic has barely started to brown and the rice has gone from translucent to white or light brown in color.

Carefully add the tomatillo mixture—it will spatter a bit, so take care! Stir to combine, then reduce the heat to low, cover, and cook without opening the lid for 20 to 25 minutes. (If the low setting on your burner runs hot, aim for 20 minutes. If it's a true low flame, shoot for 25.) All the liquid should be absorbed and the rice should be fluffy, if not, cover and let it cook another 5 to 10 minutes on low to achieve this. Turn the burner off and let the rice sit, covered, for 10 to 15 minutes more.

Taste the rice and adjust the seasoning with salt as needed. Stir in the butter and fluff the rice with a fork. Right before serving, drain the marinated tomatillos, then scatter them over the rice. Sprinkle with the remaining lime juice and enjoy!

Roasted Butternut Squash Risotto

SERVES 2 TO 4

I have two tips for making risotto: 1) Taste it frequently. 2) If you've reached the end and it looks just a bit too runny, it's perfect!

Frequent tasting ensures the seasoning is on point, of course, but it also lets you monitor the doneness of the rice. The rice should just barely have a bite to it in the end (al dente isn't just for pasta!), so don't go overboard and cook it to mush. Keep in mind the rice will continue to soak up liquid once you've finished cooking, so if you find the rice done but it still looks a bit too loose and soupy, just let it hang out for a minute or two and it'll be the perfect consistency. **VEG, GF**

---

1 medium butternut squash, peeled and diced into ¼-inch cubes (about 2½ cups)
4 tablespoons olive oil, plus more for serving
1 teaspoon dried sage
1 teaspoon dried thyme
Kosher salt
4 tablespoons (½ stick) butter
15 to 20 fresh sage leaves
1 medium shallot, finely diced
2 garlic cloves, minced
1 cup uncooked Arborio rice
1 cup dry white wine
About 4 cups vegetable stock, kept warm
2 tablespoons mascarpone cheese (optional)
1 to 2 teaspoons red wine vinegar or white wine vinegar
¼ cup freshly grated Pecorino Romano cheese, plus more shaved for serving
¼ cup roasted salted pepitas

Preheat the oven to 400°F. Line a baking sheet with aluminum foil or parchment paper.

In a medium bowl, combine the squash, 2 tablespoons of the olive oil, the dried sage, thyme, and a hefty pinch of salt and toss to coat evenly. Spread the squash in a single layer on the prepared baking sheet. Roast for about 15 minutes, until tender and caramelized but not mushy.

Meanwhile, in a small sauté pan, heat 2 tablespoons of the butter and the remaining 2 tablespoons olive oil over medium heat until the butter has melted. Carefully add the sage leaves and cook, stirring frequently, until crispy and fragrant, 2 to 3 minutes. Use a slotted spoon or small strainer to transfer the sage leaves to a paper towel, then sprinkle with a bit of salt. Pour the oil-butter mixture into a large straight-sided pan or Dutch oven and heat over medium heat. Add the shallot and cook until translucent and fragrant, about 2 minutes. You don't want the shallot to color, so reduce the heat as needed. Add the garlic and cook just until it is fragrant and the raw garlic taste has cooked out, about 1 minute more.

Add the rice and stir with a wooden spoon. Cook, stirring continuously, until the rice has barely turned from opaque to a light white/cream color all over, 1 to 2 minutes. Still stirring continuously, slowly pour in the wine and cook until it has been almost entirely absorbed by the rice.

Recipe continues

Begin adding the warm stock, one or two ladlefuls at a time, stirring almost continuously and allowing each addition of stock to be almost entirely absorbed by the rice before adding more. After the third addition of stock, season the rice with salt. Continue adding stock until the rice is creamy and cooked through but just barely has a bite to the center, 18 to 20 minutes. (At this point, the risotto should have the consistency of a chowder or runny yogurt; it will firm up and absorb more liquid as it rests.)

Remove from the heat, then add the roasted squash, mascarpone (if using), vinegar, and remaining 2 tablespoons butter and stir until the butter has melted completely. Stir in the pecorino, then taste and adjust the seasoning as needed.

Divvy up the risotto into shallow bowls, then top with the fried sage leaves, additional pecorino, a light drizzle of olive oil, and the pepitas and dig in!

Black Bean and Plantain Rice Bowl

WITH CREAMY CHIMICHURRI AND PICKLED CABBAGE

MAKES 4 BOWLS

On social media, I'm often asked for recipes for filling bowls that will keep all week long for lunch or breakfast prep. I developed this recipe to meet those requests. All these items can be made ahead "meal-prep" style and stored in the fridge for a few days—all you need to do is reheat and assemble for a quick lunch or dinner. Add some roasted chicken or seared salmon for an extra hit of protein. When selecting plantains, look for ones that are deep yellow with some dark brown spots on them and a bit of give when you gently squeeze them. Those will be the perfect mix of filling and starchy, but still a bit sweet. **VEG, V, DF, GF**

PICKLED RED CABBAGE

¼ small head red cabbage, shaved on a mandoline or by hand
⅓ cup red wine vinegar
2 tablespoons sugar
Pinch of red pepper flakes
Kosher salt

CREAMY CHIMICHURRI

1 cup tightly packed fresh cilantro
½ ripe Hass avocado
¼ cup olive oil
1 small jalapeño, coarsely chopped
2 tablespoons red wine vinegar
1 tablespoon fresh thyme leaves
2 garlic cloves, smashed and peeled
½ teaspoon ground cumin
½ teaspoon red pepper flakes
Kosher salt

GARLICKY RICE

2 tablespoons olive oil
3 garlic cloves, minced
1 cup uncooked sushi rice, rinsed well
Kosher salt

Make the cabbage: In a bowl, combine the cabbage, vinegar, sugar, red pepper flakes, and some salt. Mix well, cover, and refrigerate for at least 30 minutes or up to 24 hours.

Make the chimichurri: In a food processor or blender, combine the cilantro, avocado, olive oil, jalapeño, vinegar, thyme, garlic, cumin, and red pepper flakes. Process until smooth, 60 to 90 seconds. Season with salt to taste, cover, and refrigerate.

Make the rice: In a medium saucepan with a lid, heat the olive oil over medium heat until it ripples. Add the garlic and cook until fragrant and just barely beginning to turn brown, 2 to 3 minutes. Stir in the rice and cook for 1 to 2 minutes more, until rice begins to turn from translucent to white. Add water according to the package directions and a pinch of salt. Bring to a boil, then reduce the heat to low, cover, and simmer until the rice is tender, 15 to 20 minutes. Fluff with a fork before serving.

Meanwhile, make the plantains and beans: In a large skillet, heat the olive oil over medium heat until it ripples. Add the plantains, cut-side down, and cook until fragrant, golden brown, and cooked through but not mushy, 2 to 3 minutes per side. Transfer to a plate and tent with aluminum foil to keep warm.

Recipe and ingredients continue

PLANTAINS AND BEANS

¼ cup olive oil
2 medium-ripe large plantains, peeled and cut into 1-inch chunks
1 small red onion, sliced into half-moons
1 red bell pepper, cut into 2-inch-long matchsticks
1 jalapeño, thinly sliced into rings
1 (15-ounce) can black beans, drained and rinsed
Kosher salt

FOR SERVING

A few cilantro sprigs
½ ripe Hass avocado, sliced
Lime wedges

In the same skillet (no need to wipe it out), combine the onion, bell pepper, and jalapeño. Cook over medium-high heat until softened and just barely browning on the edges, about 5 minutes. Add the beans and cook just until heated through, 2 to 3 minutes. Taste and season with salt.

Divide the garlicky rice among four bowls. Top each bowl with the plantains, bean mixture, and pickled red cabbage. Garnish with a few cilantro sprigs and avocado slices. Drizzle with the chimichurri and serve with lime wedges alongside for squeezing.

Ryan's Brekkie Beans

SERVES 4 TO 6

Americans sleep on beans as a breakfast food, so after getting permission from the husband to share his secrets, I included this recipe in the hopes that more of you will enjoy a cozy bowl of bacony, peppery beans as a filling way to start your day. Ryan uses dry pinto beans for this recipe, which do require presoaking, so be sure to build in time for that. You can use two cans of cooked pinto beans in place of making your own, but Ryan does caution the beans won't be quite as *extra*. **GF**

---

2 cups dried pinto beans, or 2 (15-ounce) cans pinto beans, drained and rinsed
2 slices bacon, cut into 1-inch pieces
1 small white onion, cut into 1-inch pieces
1 green bell pepper, cut into 1-inch pieces
1 jalapeño, halved lengthwise
4 garlic cloves, smashed and peeled
2 sprigs epazote (optional, but highly encouraged!)
1 tablespoon chicken bouillon powder, or 1 bouillon cube
Pinch of red pepper flakes
Kosher salt and freshly ground black pepper

FOR SERVING
Fried eggs
Charred corn tortillas
Crumbled queso fresco
Chopped fresh cilantro

If using dried beans, rinse them under cold water and pick out any stones or debris, then place them in a large bowl with cold water to cover and let soak for at least 2 hours or up to overnight.

Place the bacon in a large Dutch oven, then cook over medium heat, stirring occasionally, until some of the fat has rendered and the bacon has begun to brown but not turn crisp, 3 to 5 minutes. Add the onion, bell pepper, jalapeño, and garlic. Cook until the edges of all the aromatics begin to brown and the onion has turned slightly translucent, 6 to 8 minutes.

Drain the beans, then add them to the pot, along with enough fresh water to cover them by about 1 inch. Stir in the epazote (if using), bouillon, red pepper flakes, and some salt. Bring to a boil, then reduce the heat to low and cover the pot with the lid ajar. Simmer, stirring occasionally, until the beans are tender but not mushy, 1 to 1½ hours, adding water as needed to keep the beans submerged as they cook. (If you're using canned beans, add the drained and rinsed beans to the pot, along with 2 cups water. Stir in the epazote, bouillon, red pepper flakes, and salt and cook over medium heat at a low simmer until the onions and bell pepper have softened and the water has reduced by about one-third, 20 to 30 minutes.)

Taste and adjust the seasoning with salt and black pepper as needed (we go heavy-handed with the pepper in our home!). Serve these with a fried egg, charred tortillas, crumbled queso fresco, and some cilantro—an iconic breakfast, honestly.

Sautéed Kale Pesto Butter Beans

SERVES 4 TO 6

The millennial in me adores a kale salad, and I'm always looking for new ways to eat it. This recipe uses the hearty green as a base for pesto, which gives it a rich, earthy flavor. Adding some quickly sautéed kale to the bean mixture creates added texture and bite, as well as another layer of kale flavor. The result is a filling yet bright bean dish that most definitely belongs in your rotation. The ice in the pesto may surprise you, but it helps to emulsify the mixture and preserve its green color by maintaining a low temperature while the blades run. **VEG, GF**

KALE PESTO

1 bunch lacinato kale, leaves stemmed and coarsely chopped
½ cup packed fresh basil leaves
½ cup pine nuts (pistachios or Marcona almonds work fine, too), toasted
½ cup freshly grated Parmigiano-Reggiano cheese
4 garlic cloves, smashed and peeled
1 teaspoon red pepper flakes
2 ice cubes
½ to ¾ cup extra-virgin olive oil
Kosher salt and freshly ground black pepper

BEANS

2 tablespoons olive oil
2 or 3 garlic cloves, chopped
1 bunch lacinato kale, leaves stemmed and thinly sliced
2 (14.25-ounce) cans butter beans, drained and rinsed
Kosher salt and freshly ground black pepper

FOR SERVING

Shaved Parmigiano-Reggiano cheese
12 to 15 small fresh basil leaves
Extra-virgin olive oil

Make the pesto: In a food processor, combine the kale, basil, pine nuts, cheese, garlic, red pepper flakes, and ice cubes. Pulse a few times until it's all coarsely chopped. With the motor running, slowly drizzle in the olive oil until the pesto reaches a thick, pastelike consistency (you may not need all the oil). Taste and season with salt and pepper.

Make the beans: In a large skillet, heat the olive oil over medium heat until it ripples. Add the garlic and cook until fragrant and just starting to brown, about 2 minutes. Add the kale and cook until just barely wilted, 2 to 3 minutes, then stir in the beans. Cook until the kale has wilted a bit more and the beans are fully heated through, 2 to 3 minutes more. Add the pesto and cook, stirring, to ensure the mixture is evenly coated and heated through, 2 to 3 minutes more. Taste and adjust the seasoning with salt and pepper as needed.

Transfer the sautéed kale and butter beans to a serving dish. Garnish with shaved cheese, basil leaves, and a glug of olive oil, then serve.

English Pea Farro

WITH CRISPY SHIITAKE MUSHROOM BACON

SERVES 4 TO 6

This mushroom "bacon" was a recipe I used frequently back in my cooking competition days. It's a quick way to add an unexpected hit of umami and crisp texture. The key is to slice the shiitakes as thinly and evenly as possible, so take your time; otherwise, they won't crisp up the same. While I love this dish all year round, I prefer waiting for early spring peas, which have tender sweetness and slight starchiness. VEG

3 to 4 tablespoons olive oil, plus more for serving
1 small leek, white and light green parts only, thinly sliced into half-moons and washed well
1 cup dry farro, rinsed
Kosher salt
4 ounces shiitake mushrooms, stemmed and very thinly sliced
1 tablespoon low-sodium soy sauce or coconut aminos
1 pound fresh or frozen English peas (about 3 cups)
1½ cups whole milk
4 tablespoons (½ stick) butter
2 tablespoons coarsely chopped fresh tarragon, plus whole leaves for serving (optional)
Zest and juice of ½ lemon
Freshly ground black pepper
Handful of pea shoots, for serving (optional, but highly encouraged in springtime!)

In a medium pot, combine 1 tablespoon of the olive oil, the leek, and farro and cook over medium heat, stirring frequently, until the farro is toasty and fragrant and the leek is just taking on some color, about 5 minutes. Add enough water to cover the farro by about 2 inches, then add a hefty pinch of salt. Bring to a boil, then reduce the heat to low and simmer, uncovered, until the farro is tender with a bit of chew to it, 25 to 30 minutes. Drain any excess water, then transfer the farro to a bowl and cover.

Preheat the oven to 325°F. Line a baking sheet with parchment paper.

Place the shiitakes in a large bowl. Drizzle with the remaining 2 to 3 tablespoons olive oil and the soy sauce, and season generously with salt. Toss well to coat, then dump the shiitakes onto the prepared baking sheet and arrange in a single layer. Bake for 15 to 20 minutes, stirring them halfway through the cooking time, until the shiitakes are a deep rich brown and crisped through.

In a medium pot, combine half of the peas, the milk, and a pinch of salt. Bring to a simmer over medium-high heat and cook until just tender, 8 to 10 minutes for fresh, 3 to 4 minutes for frozen. Transfer the mixture to a blender and blend on high speed until totally smooth, 1 to 2 minutes.

Pour the pea mixture into a medium pot and add the farro and remaining uncooked peas. Cook over medium heat, stirring frequently, until the sauce has thickened and the whole peas are slightly softened, 5 to 7 minutes. Remove from the heat and add the butter, chopped tarragon, lemon zest, and lemon juice. Stir well to combine, then taste and adjust the seasoning with salt and pepper.

Divide the farro among individual bowls, or serve in a large shallow bowl. Top with the shiitake bacon, a drizzle of olive oil, and if desired, a few whole tarragon leaves and some fresh pea shoots.

Cheesy Breakfast Oatmeal

WITH BROWN-BUTTER EGGS AND OVEN BACON

SERVES 4 TO 6

During my first visit to Copenhagen, a local took me to a tiny hole-in-the wall restaurant called Grød that only served porridges. From farro to risotto, the menu was full of cozy bowls, but the one that caught my eye was a savory, cheesy oatmeal breakfast bowl. Until then, I had never even considered oatmeal a savory dish, but I ordered it anyway and was so pleased. The oats provided a great canvas for all the other traditional breakfast toppings. It was *just* the dish I needed to keep me going that chilly Copenhagen winter morning. I hope you like my riff on their dish as much as I do.

8 slices thick-cut applewood-smoked bacon
3 tablespoons olive oil
1 small shallot, minced
2 garlic cloves, minced
1½ cups rolled oats
2½ cups chicken stock or vegetable stock
2 cups whole milk, plus more as needed
4 large handfuls baby spinach (about 4 cups)
Kosher salt and freshly ground black pepper
2 tablespoons butter
4 to 6 large eggs
1½ cups ¼-inch cubes sharp cheddar cheese

Feeling a little bit EXTRA?

Swap the regular bacon for miso-glazed bacon—the recipe is on the next page! (Note that if you prepare this with miso-glazed bacon, the recipe will not be gluten-free.)

Preheat the oven to 400°F. Line a baking sheet with parchment paper.

Arrange the bacon on the baking sheet in a single layer. Bake for 15 to 20 minutes, until crispy. Remove from the oven and transfer the bacon to a paper towel–lined plate; reserve the rendered fat.

Meanwhile, in a large pot or Dutch oven, heat 2 tablespoons of the olive oil over medium heat until it ripples. Add the shallot and garlic and cook until fragrant and translucent but not quite browning, 2 to 3 minutes. Add the oats and pour in the stock and milk and bring the mixture to a boil, then reduce the heat to low. Simmer, stirring occasionally, until the oats are tender and creamy, 25 to 30 minutes.

In a large nonstick skillet or sauté pan, heat the remaining 1 tablespoon olive oil over medium-high heat until it ripples and the pan is nearly smoking. Throw in the spinach and a heavy pinch each of salt and pepper and cook, stirring continuously, until the spinach has wilted to about one-quarter of its original volume, about 1 minute. Transfer the spinach to a plate or bowl and return the pan to the heat. Add the butter and cook until it begins to foam and turn a light golden brown.

Crack the eggs into the skillet one at a time. Cook the eggs for about 2 minutes, then start spooning the brown butter over each of them. (I like the eggs runny, but cook them to your desired doneness.)

To finish the oats, stir in 1 cup of the cheese, 1 to 2 tablespoons of bacon fat, and some salt and pepper and mix until the cheese has melted and is fully incorporated.

To serve, chop or tear the cooked bacon into bite-size pieces. Divide the oatmeal among bowls, then top with the bacon, some cooked spinach, and one of the butter-basted eggs. Sprinkle with the remaining cheddar cubes and season with additional salt and pepper, if desired.

Miso-Glazed Millionaire's Bacon

MAKES 8 PIECES

8 slices thick-cut applewood-smoked bacon
1 tablespoon butter, melted
1 tablespoon dark brown sugar
1 tablespoon light miso paste
Small pinch of cayenne pepper
Freshly ground black pepper

Preheat the oven to 400°F. Line a baking sheet with parchment paper or aluminum foil. Lay the bacon on the prepared pan in a single layer. In a small bowl, stir together the melted butter, brown sugar, miso, cayenne, and a generous amount of black pepper to combine. Use a small spoon to spread the mixture evenly over the bacon, ensuring each slice is evenly coated. Bake for 12 to 15 minutes, until well caramelized and crisp.

Toasty Pistachio Quinoa

WITH HONEYED HALLOUMI

SERVES 4 TO 6

This dish is my favorite way to enjoy quinoa, which so often suffers a boring fate. The quinoa can easily be made in a rice cooker if you prefer, but make sure to keep it warm as this salad is best enjoyed when the residual heat from the quinoa gently wilts the arugula and keeps the sweet and salty Halloumi from getting cold. **VEG, GF**

---

2 cups vegetable stock or water
1 cup uncooked white quinoa, rinsed
1 tablespoon ground coriander
Kosher salt
2 large handfuls of baby arugula (about 3 cups)
1 cup loosely packed fresh mint leaves
2 Persian cucumbers, thinly sliced into rounds
3 or 4 small radishes, thinly sliced
Zest and juice of 1 lemon
3 tablespoons olive oil
Freshly ground black pepper
2 tablespoons butter
2 (4-ounce) blocks Halloumi cheese, cut into 4 slices per block and patted dry
½ cup coarsely chopped raw pistachios
2 tablespoons honey
1 teaspoon red pepper flakes

In a medium pot with a lid, combine the stock, quinoa, coriander, and a hefty pinch of salt. Bring to a boil over medium-high heat, then reduce the heat to low, cover, and simmer until the quinoa is cooked through and the liquid has been absorbed, 15 to 20 minutes. Remove from the heat but keep the pot covered so the quinoa stays warm.

Meanwhile, in a large bowl, combine the arugula, mint, cucumbers, and radishes. Add the lemon zest, lemon juice, and olive oil. Season with salt and pepper. Toss gently to combine. Refrigerate until ready to serve.

In a medium nonstick sauté pan or well-seasoned cast-iron pan, melt the butter over medium heat. When the butter has just begun to turn brown, add the Halloumi and cook, undisturbed, until it's a nice golden brown color on the bottom, 2 to 3 minutes. Flip the Halloumi over, then sprinkle the pistachios all around the pan. Cook the Halloumi and pistachios until the cheese is browned well on the second side and the pistachios are toasted and aromatic, 2 to 3 minutes more. Drizzle the honey all over the pan and stir well to coat the nuts and cheese. Cook for a minute or two to evenly coat everything with the honey, then remove from the heat and sprinkle with a generous pinch of salt and the red pepper flakes.

Fluff the warm quinoa with a fork, then dump it into the bowl with the arugula mixture. Mix until combined, then taste and adjust the seasoning.

Arrange the quinoa on a serving platter or individual plates, then top with the Halloumi. Spoon over the honey and pistachio mixture from the pan. Serve while the quinoa and Halloumi are still warm.

SIDES

Broccoli Rabe

WITH CRISPY GARLIC AND LEMON DRESSING

SERVES 2 TO 4

The contrast of crisp, toasty garlic with acidic lemon and bitter broccoli rabe is such a delight. This versatile recipe is great to keep up your sleeve for a quick dinner party side dish since the flavor-to-effort ratio can't be beat. When blanching bitter greens, I like to put a heavy pinch of both sugar *and* salt in the water—it helps mellow out some of the broccoli rabe's bitterness. **VEG, V, DF, GF**

3 or 4 garlic cloves, peeled
½ cup olive oil
½ lemon, thinly sliced and seeded
1 tablespoon chopped fresh mint
1 tablespoon chopped fresh basil
1 teaspoon red pepper flakes
1 teaspoon kosher salt, plus more as needed
½ teaspoon freshly ground black pepper
Pinch of sugar
1 bunch broccoli rabe, bottom inch trimmed off
Flaky sea salt, for serving

Slice the garlic as thin as you can on a mandoline or by hand into even slices. (If they are different thicknesses, they won't brown or crisp up evenly.)

In a small pot, heat the olive oil over low heat until it ripples. Add the garlic and cook, stirring occasionally, until evenly brown and crispy, about 2 minutes. Drain the garlic in a fine-mesh strainer set over a heatproof container and reserve the garlic oil. Spread the garlic chips on a paper towel to drain and cool.

Return the garlic oil to the pot and set it over medium heat. Carefully place the lemon slices in the oil (it may spatter!) and cook until they have begun to fall apart and are very fragrant, 2 to 3 minutes. Pour the lemon-oil mixture into a heatproof medium bowl. Add the mint, basil, red pepper flakes, kosher salt, and black pepper. Mix well to combine.

Bring a large pot of heavily salted water to a boil over high heat. Add the sugar and let it dissolve, then toss in the broccoli rabe. Cook until the leaves are a nice deep green and the stalks are a vibrant bright green and tender but still have a bit of a bite to them, about 3 minutes. Immediately drain the broccoli rabe in a colander, shaking it to remove as much excess water as you can.

Arrange the broccoli rabe on a serving platter. Add the garlic chips to the lemony sauce and mix well. Spoon enough sauce over the broccoli rabe to dress it all, then finish with a pinch of flaky salt. Serve hot, with any remaining sauce on the side—you're gonna want it!

Charred Green Beans

WITH GINGER TOMATO JAM

SERVES 4 TO 6

This gingery tomato jam was an accompaniment to a gold medal–winning dish we served at the 2012 Culinary Olympics. With that pedigree, it has been a mainstay in my repertoire ever since. The gentle spice and brightness from the ginger make it a great companion for anything from these green beans to a simple grilled fish. This is a great dish for your vegetarian friends when it's made without the optional fish sauce. But if you're not veggie, I highly recommend adding it. **VEG, GF, DF**

JAM

1 pound ripe (but not soft) beefsteak or Roma (plum) tomatoes, cored, seeded, and coarsely chopped into ¼-inch pieces
½ cup apple cider vinegar
½ cup lightly packed light brown sugar
½ cup honey
1 tablespoon minced or grated fresh ginger
1 star anise pod
1 cinnamon stick
1 teaspoon fish sauce (optional)
½ teaspoon ground turmeric
Kosher salt and freshly ground black pepper

BEANS

1 tablespoon olive oil, plus more for greasing
1 pound green beans
1 tablespoon honey
1 tablespoon white sesame seeds
1 teaspoon toasted sesame oil
Kosher salt

Make the jam: In a medium pot, combine the tomatoes, vinegar, brown sugar, honey, ginger, star anise, cinnamon, fish sauce (if using), and turmeric. Stir everything well, then cook over medium heat, stirring frequently, until the tomatoes are soft but not mushy, the liquid has reduced almost completely, and the mixture has a thick, glossy consistency, 10 to 20 minutes, depending on the temperature of your stove and the ripeness of your tomatoes.

Remove from the heat and season with salt and pepper. Transfer to a medium bowl, cover loosely, and let stand at room temperature while you cook the beans.

Make the beans: Place an oven rack in the highest position and preheat the broiler to high. Line a large baking sheet with aluminum foil, then grease it with olive oil.

In a large bowl, combine the green beans, olive oil, honey, sesame seeds, sesame oil, and a heavy pinch of salt. Toss the beans well to evenly coat, then arrange them in an even layer on the prepared baking sheet. Pop them under the broiler. Start checking the beans after 2 to 3 minutes. They should have some nice charred spots on the outside, but still have a bit of a crunch when you bite into them; keep a close eye on them to prevent burning.

Transfer the beans to a serving platter. Just before serving, dot the jam all over the beans and serve with any extra jam on the side. (You can store leftover jam in an airtight container in the refrigerator for up to 2 weeks, but believe me, it won't last that long.)

Grilled Broccolini

WITH HONEYED RICOTTA AND MINTY JALAPEÑO DRIZZLE

SERVES 4 TO 6

One hill I will absolutely die on: We all need to be putting more mint in savory food—and if you don't agree with me, this broccolini recipe will change your mind. The char on the broccolini and creamy ricotta need a lil' extra push to balance everything out, and mint is just the herb for the job. Adding some spicy jalapeño and honey rounds everything out into the perfect grilled veggie recipe. **VEG, GF**

DRIZZLE

2 tablespoons olive oil
1 jalapeño, minced
Zest of ½ lemon
Juice of 1 lemon
1 tablespoon chopped fresh mint
1 garlic clove, grated or minced
Kosher salt and freshly ground black pepper

BROCCOLINI AND RICOTTA

2 bunches broccolini, stalks trimmed to uniform size
¼ cup olive oil
Kosher salt and freshly ground black pepper
8 ounces (1 cup) whole-milk ricotta cheese, homemade (recipe follows) or store-bought
2 tablespoons honey
2 teaspoons whole black peppercorns or peppercorn mix, toasted and cracked

Make the drizzle: In a small bowl, stir together the olive oil, jalapeño, lemon zest, lemon juice, mint, and garlic. Season with salt and pepper, cover, and refrigerate.

Make the broccolini and ricotta: Preheat a grill to high for about 10 minutes.

Rub the broccolini with the olive oil and season with salt and ground pepper. Carefully place the broccolini on the grill in an even layer and cook until the broccolini is tender and has some good charring but is not burnt or mushy, 1 to 2 minutes per side. Remove from the grill.

In a small bowl, stir together the ricotta, honey, cracked pepper, and a generous pinch of salt. Spread the ricotta mixture over a serving dish, then arrange the grilled broccolini on top. Hit it with the minty jalapeño drizzle right before serving.

Make your own ricotta—the recipe is on the next page!

Homemade Ricotta Cheese

MAKES ABOUT 2 CUPS

- 4 cups whole milk (not ultrapasteurized)
- 1 cup heavy cream, plus more as needed
- 1 teaspoon kosher salt, plus more as needed
- 2½ tablespoons fresh lemon juice
- 2 tablespoons distilled white vinegar

In a medium saucepan with a lid, combine the milk, cream, and salt and bring to a low simmer over medium heat. When the temperature hits between 180° and 185°F, add the lemon juice and vinegar and turn off the heat. Stir for 3 seconds, then cover and let stand for 10 minutes, undisturbed. Line a colander with cheesecloth or a clean thin kitchen towel and set it over a large bowl, then pour the milk mixture into it. Let stand for 5 to 10 minutes for a creamy ricotta, or longer for a thicker cheese. For a thinner, creamier consistency, stir in a bit more cream. Taste and adjust the seasoning with more salt as needed. Store the ricotta in an airtight container in the refrigerator for up to 5 days.

Phyllo-Baked Asparagus

WITH TRUFFLED EGG SAUCE

SERVES 4 TO 6

Working with phyllo can be intimidating, but so long as you keep the dough cold and covered, you'll find it's actually satisfying to work with and offers a way to add textural complexity to dishes. Here thin pieces of phyllo are wrapped around asparagus and baked to glassy perfection. The key is using plenty of butter and only wrapping the bundles two times around for a super-crisp bake. The truffled egg sauce is my version of a French sauce called gibriche, which I think you'll agree deserves a spot on your next crudités board. VEG

SAUCE

2 large eggs
1 small shallot, minced
2 tablespoons minced capers
2 tablespoons minced cornichons
1 tablespoon finely chopped fresh dill
1 tablespoon chopped fresh tarragon
1 tablespoon whole-grain or stone-ground mustard
1 garlic clove, grated or minced
¾ cup olive oil
1 to 2 teaspoons truffle oil
Kosher salt and freshly ground black pepper

ASPARAGUS

1 (16-ounce) package frozen phyllo dough, thawed per the package directions
½ cup (1 stick) butter, melted
2 bunches medium-thick asparagus (about 24 stalks), ends trimmed
Flaky sea salt

Preheat the oven to 400°F. Line a baking sheet with parchment paper or aluminum foil.

Make the sauce: Bring a small saucepan of water to a rolling boil over high heat. Add the eggs and cook for exactly 10 minutes. Drain the eggs and run them under cold water to stop the cooking. When the eggs are cool enough to handle, peel them and chop them evenly into ⅛-inch pieces.

Meanwhile, in a medium bowl, whisk together the shallot, capers, cornichons, dill, tarragon, mustard, and garlic to combine. Add the eggs, olive oil, truffle oil, and some kosher salt and pepper and gently mix to combine. (I like it to be more of a broken, oil-based sauce, but if you whisk it vigorously and break up the egg, it will start to emulsify and become a more chunky aïoli-style sauce—your call!) Cover and let stand at room temperature until you're ready to serve the asparagus.

Make the asparagus: Lay one sheet of phyllo dough on a clean surface and brush generously with melted butter. Place another sheet of phyllo dough on top and brush again with butter. Keep any phyllo you're not working with covered with a kitchen towel so it doesn't dry out.

Use your asparagus stalks as a guide to measure and cut the phyllo into rectangles that are roughly 4 × 8 inches; you'll need 7 to 10 sheets. Take 3 pieces of asparagus and place them on top of a phyllo rectangle, leaving about 1 inch of the stems and 2 to 3 inches of the tips overhanging the phyllo. Tightly roll up the phyllo around the asparagus so it makes a

Recipe continues

nice bundle. Trim any excess phyllo so there are no more than two layers of phyllo, then place the roll seam-side down on the prepared baking sheet. Repeat until all the asparagus has been bundled. Space the bundles evenly on the baking sheet.

Brush the asparagus tips and the tops of the phyllo with any remaining melted butter and sprinkle with flaky salt. Bake for 15 to 20 minutes, until the phyllo is golden brown and crispy all over. Remove from the oven and let cool for 5 minutes.

Arrange the asparagus bundles on a serving platter. Place the truffled egg sauce in a serving bowl next to the asparagus for dunking or drizzling and serve! Store any leftover sauce in an airtight container in the refrigerator for up to 5 days. Bring to room temperature before serving (the olive oil will solidify when cold).

Feeling a little bit EXTRA?

Add some prosciutto! When you assemble the bundles, wrap the asparagus with a piece of prosciutto before wrapping them with the phyllo for a salty, savory addition to this recipe. Naturally, this recipe is no longer vegetarian with the addition of prosciutto, but it's equally delish with (as shown at left) or without!

Roasted and Dressed Brussels Sprouts

SERVES 4 TO 6

I love a dish that explores the duality of a product by preparing it in two completely different ways. Here, we use the outer leaves of the Brussels sprout (that so many people tragically discard!) and give them a quick blanch, rendering them perfectly tender with a vibrant green color. The leaves get tossed with sweet raisins and Manchego cheese, then topped with the caramelized sweet and garlicky cores of the Brussels. **VEG, GF**

Kosher salt
2 pounds large Brussels sprouts
4 tablespoons olive oil
2 tablespoons balsamic vinegar
2 garlic cloves, grated or minced
1 tablespoon honey
1 teaspoon garlic powder
Small pinch of red pepper flakes
Freshly ground black pepper
2 ounces 6-to-12-month-aged Manchego cheese, shaved (about ¾ cup)
½ cup golden raisins, soaked in hot water for 10 to 15 minutes, then drained
½ cup fresh parsley leaves
Zest and juice of ½ lemon

Preheat the oven to 375°F. Line a baking sheet with aluminum foil or parchment paper.

Bring a large pot of heavily salted water to a heavy rolling boil.

Cut a tiny bit of the root end of the Brussels sprouts. Remove some of the bright green outer leaves and place them in a medium bowl. Use a paring knife to cut off more of the root end and peel off a few more leaves. Reserve about half the leaves from each sprout, placing the outer leaves in one bowl and the tender core in a separate bowl. If the cores are very large, cut the cores in half.

To the bowl with the Brussels sprout cores, add 2 tablespoons of the olive oil, the vinegar, honey, grated garlic, garlic powder, and red pepper flakes. Season with salt and lots of black pepper and toss well to coat. Evenly spread the cores over the prepared baking sheet and bake for 15 to 20 minutes, stirring every 5 minutes, until they are nicely browned and tender and the honey and garlic have caramelized.

Meanwhile, fill a large bowl with ice and water and set it near the stovetop. Add the reserved Brussels sprout leaves to the boiling water and give it a quick stir. Blanch until the leaves have turned a nice bright green and are slightly tender but still hold their shape fairly well, 1 to 2 minutes. Immediately drain and place them in the ice bath to cool completely. Drain the leaves and dry them super well, ideally in a salad spinner or by laying them out on a kitchen towel and dabbing them dry.

In a large bowl, combine the blanched leaves, the remaining 2 tablespoons olive oil, the cheese, raisins, parsley, lemon zest, and lemon juice. Season heavily with salt and lots of black pepper. Toss well to combine, then taste and adjust the seasoning as needed. Transfer to a serving dish and top with the warm roasted Brussels sprout cores just before serving.

Roasted Baby Carrots

WITH CHARRED PIPIÁN SALSA AND COTIJA CHEESE

SERVES 4 TO 6

Pipián is a traditional Mexican sauce with a base of pepitas (roasted hulled pumpkin seeds) and tomatillos. It's a wonderful introduction to the style of salsas often seen in the southern parts of Mexico that expertly blend nuts, seeds, fruits, and herbs into complex and luscious accompaniments. Pipián is often served with chicken, but here it's drizzled over roasted baby carrots for an ideal fall side dish. If you have any left over, which I doubt you will, it'll keep well in an airtight container in the fridge for up to a week. **VEG, GF**

SALSA

1 poblano pepper
1 jalapeño
4 small tomatillos, husked and rinsed well
4 garlic cloves, smashed and peeled
½ large white onion, chopped into 1-inch pieces
1 tablespoon neutral oil
1 cup packed fresh cilantro, coarsely chopped, plus whole leaves for garnish
¾ cup roasted pepitas, plus more for garnish
2 to 3 tablespoons chopped fresh epazote (optional, but highly encouraged!)
½ cup vegetable stock or water, plus more as needed
Kosher salt

CARROTS

2 pounds small organic bunched baby carrots, tops removed
3 tablespoons olive oil
1 tablespoon ground coriander
1 teaspoon ground cumin
Kosher salt
2 to 3 ounces crumbled Cotija cheese, for garnish

Make the salsa: Preheat the broiler to high. Line two baking sheets with aluminum foil.

Arrange the poblano, jalapeño, tomatillos, garlic, and onion in a single layer on one of the prepared baking sheets, then rub them all over with the neutral oil. Broil the vegetables for 5 to 8 minutes, turning occasionally, until lightly charred and blistered all over. Let cool slightly. Adjust the oven temperature to 425°F.

When the vegetables are cool enough to handle, stem, peel, and seed the poblano and remove the stem from the jalapeño. Transfer the poblano and jalapeño to a food processor along with the charred tomatillos, garlic, and onion, then add the cilantro, pepitas, and epazote (if using). With the motor running, drizzle in ½ cup of the stock and process until smooth. Taste and season with salt. Adjust the consistency with additional stock or water as needed—it should be somewhere between Caesar dressing and hummus. Cover and let stand at room temperature.

Make the carrots: In a large bowl, toss the carrots with the olive oil, coriander, cumin, and some salt until evenly coated. Spread the carrots in a single layer on the second prepared baking sheet. Roast for 20 to 25 minutes, turning once halfway through the cooking time, until tender and slightly caramelized.

To serve, arrange the roasted carrots on a large serving platter and dollop with the salsa. Garnish with cilantro leaves, more pepitas, and the cheese, and make sure to serve any extra salsa on the side for dunking!

Bacon-Braised Belgian Endives

SERVES 4

The bitter greens girlie in me loves this recipe so dang much. It's rich without being heavy and the endive's slight bitterness balances out the decadence of the bacon perfectly. Top it with a hit of lemon juice and zest and you're in business. If you can't find red endive, white is fine, too—I just find the colored endive to be more of a showstopper.

2 tablespoons olive oil
4 heads red Belgian endive, halved lengthwise
Kosher salt
1 medium shallot, finely diced
3 slices bacon, cut into ½-inch pieces
2 garlic cloves, smashed and peeled
1 tablespoon butter
1 tablespoon all-purpose flour
1 cup chicken stock or vegetable stock
¼ cup red wine vinegar
Freshly ground black pepper
4 thyme sprigs
Fresh lemon zest and juice
Flaky sea salt

Preheat the oven to 300°F.

In a large cast-iron or other heavy-duty oven-safe skillet, heat the olive oil over medium-high heat until it ripples. Season the cut side of the endives with a pinch of kosher salt, then carefully place them cut-side down in the pan. Cook, undisturbed, until nicely browned on the bottom, about 3 minutes. Transfer to a plate or baking sheet.

Reduce the heat to medium and add the shallot, bacon, and garlic to the pan. Cook, stirring now and then, until the bacon begins to brown and crisp just on the edges, about 2 minutes. Add the butter and let it melt, then add the flour and cook, stirring continuously, for 1 minute to lightly toast the flour and coat the aromatics and bacon. Add the stock and vinegar and stir until all the lumps of flour have dissolved. Season with kosher salt and pepper to taste.

Place the endives back in the pan, nestling them seared-side down in the liquid. Sprinkle the thyme sprigs on top, then bring to a boil. Remove from the heat, cover the pan with a lid, and place in the oven. Bake for 30 minutes, or until the endives are tender but not falling apart.

Let the endives cool for a few minutes, then flip them over to expose the seared side. Just before serving, sprinkle with some lemon zest and juice and a good pinch of flaky salt, then enjoy.

Creamy Thyme-Infused Celery Root Gratin

SERVES 4 TO 6

This dish is a mainstay on my menus around the holidays and easily wins over a traditional potato au gratin. By gently infusing the cream mixture with the fresh thyme, the dish is left with a consistent and subtle thyme flavor throughout every bite. Make sure the Gruyère on top gets nicely browned before serving! **VEG, GF**

2 tablespoons butter, plus more for greasing
3 garlic cloves, minced
1 cup heavy cream
1 cup whole milk
2 tablespoons fresh thyme leaves, plus more for garnish
1 teaspoon freshly ground black pepper, plus more as needed
3 pounds celery root, peeled, trimmed, and sliced into ⅛-inch-thick rounds
1½ cups freshly grated Gruyère cheese
¾ cup freshly grated Parmigiano-Reggiano cheese
Kosher salt
Celery leaves, for garnish (optional)

Preheat the oven to 375°F. Grease a 9 × 13-inch or large oval baking dish with butter.

In a medium saucepan, melt the butter over medium heat. Add the garlic and cook, stirring frequently, until fragrant and barely cooked but not brown, about 1 minute. Stir in the cream, milk, thyme, and pepper. Reduce the heat to medium-low and bring the mixture to a gentle simmer. Cook for 3 to 5 minutes to let the aromatics infuse the milk and cream. Watch it carefully so it doesn't boil over. Remove from the heat and let cool to room temperature.

In a large bowl, combine the celery root, 1 cup of the Gruyère, the Parmigiano, and the milk mixture. Season heavily with salt and pepper, then toss well, ensuring the celery root is evenly coated.

Shingle the celery root slices in the baking dish, layering them so there is a bit of the cheese mixture between each slice, then tap the dish on the countertop to settle all the slices into place. Pour any leftover cheese-milk mixture over the celery root, then top with the remaining ½ cup of Gruyère.

Cover the baking dish with aluminum foil and bake for 45 minutes. Remove the foil and bake for 15 to 20 minutes more, until the top is golden brown and the celery root is tender when pierced with a fork. Let the gratin cool for 10 to 15 minutes. Just before serving, garnish with thyme and some celery leaves, if desired.

Grandma's Tomato Glop

SERVES 4 TO 6

My grandma was by no means a chef. She cooked as a means to an end and had three hungry children to feed, so this "Tomato Glop" became a repeat recipe for her. In her version, day-old baguette or bread was torn into pieces and warmed through on the stove with a jar of pasta sauce, rendering the mixture into a thick, gloppy dish that, while super quick and filling, wasn't the most beautiful. I've turned her classic two-ingredient dish into an elevated side reminiscent of strata or savory bread pudding that goes perfectly with roasted chicken or pork chops—while also staying true to its roots. **VEG**

1 pound day-old sourdough bread or baguette, cut into 1-inch pieces
¼ cup olive oil, plus more as needed
Kosher salt
2 garlic cloves, finely chopped
½ medium yellow onion, diced into ½-inch pieces
3 very ripe Roma (plum) or small beefsteak tomatoes, chopped into 1-inch pieces
2 cups vegetable stock
½ teaspoon garlic powder
1 large egg
Freshly ground black pepper
¼ cup freshly grated Parmigiano-Reggiano cheese
Fresh basil, for garnish

Preheat the oven to 400°F. Line a baking sheet with paper towels and set aside.

In a large cast-iron skillet or heavy-duty baking dish, combine the bread and olive oil. Stir to coat the bread with the oil and give it a good pinch of salt. Cook over medium heat, stirring frequently, until it has taken on a light brown color on the edges but the middle of the chunks are still slightly soft, 6 to 8 minutes. Add the garlic and cook until the bread is toasty and the garlic is fragrant and light brown, another 1 to 2 minutes, then transfer to the lined baking sheet to drain.

If there's not much oil left in the pan, add a touch more, then throw in the onion and cook over medium-high heat until it starts to color on the edges, 4 to 5 minutes. Add the tomatoes and cook, stirring frequently, until the tomatoes have broken down and smell like a rich sauce, about 5 minutes. Add 1 cup of the stock, the garlic powder, and some salt and cook until the liquid has reduced by about half, 4 to 5 minutes more. Then transfer this mixture to a large bowl along with the toasted bread.

In a small bowl, whisk the egg into the remaining 1 cup stock.

Add the egg stock mixture and a hefty pinch each of salt and pepper to the toasted bread mixture and mix to coat evenly. Transfer to a large ceramic or glass baking dish, then sprinkle with the cheese and slide the pan into the oven. Bake for about 15 minutes, until the top is crusty and browned and the middle is set but still slightly jiggly and very moist.

Just before serving, sprinkle with the basil, and say thanks to Grandma Maude as you dig in!

TELQUE

Chickpea Fries

WITH WHIPPED FETA CALABRIAN CHILE DIP

SERVES 6

These panisse, or chickpea fries, are a common side dish and street food in the South of France. After spending some time setting up in the fridge, the batter is sliced into french fry-shaped batons and fried in hot oil, creating a light and crispy outside with a smooth and creamy interior. If you've never had one, you're really in for a treat, especially after dunking it in spicy whipped feta. After all—what's a fry without a good dip? **VEG, GF**

CHICKPEA FRIES

Butter, for greasing
4 cups vegetable stock
2 garlic cloves, grated or minced
1 teaspoon garlic powder
1 teaspoon smoked paprika
Zest and juice of ½ lemon
1 teaspoon kosher salt
2 cups chickpea flour, sifted

WHIPPED FETA CALABRIAN CHILE DIP

4 ounces feta cheese, crumbled
½ cup plain full-fat Greek yogurt
Zest and juice of ½ lemon
2 tablespoons minced fresh chives
1 tablespoon chopped Calabrian chiles
Kosher salt and freshly ground black pepper

About 4 cups neutral oil, for frying
Nonstick cooking spray (optional)

NOTE: Cleaning your knife between cuts and coating the blade with a bit of cooking spray will help you cut very even fries.

Make the fries: Grease a 9 × 13-inch baking sheet, then line with parchment paper.

In a large Dutch oven, whisk together the stock, garlic, garlic powder, paprika, lemon zest and juice, and salt. Gradually add the chickpea flour, whisking continuously to prevent lumps, then place the pot over medium heat. Cook, whisking frequently, until the mixture thickens (it will bubble and spit, so take care!) and pulls away from the sides of the pan, 5 to 7 minutes. It should look like very thick hummus.

Transfer the mixture to the prepared baking sheet, spreading it evenly to about ½-inch thickness. Grease a second sheet of parchment and lay it greased-side down over the chickpea flour mixture, then set another small baking sheet on top and weigh it down with a book or cans. Let cool for 30 minutes, then refrigerate for at least 1 hour or until firm.

Meanwhile, make the dip: In a food processor or blender, combine all dip ingredients. Process until smooth and creamy. Taste and season with salt and pepper, then transfer the dip to a serving bowl. Cover and refrigerate until ready to serve.

Heat the neutral oil in a large Dutch oven over medium-high heat until it reaches 375°F. Line a large baking sheet with paper towels and set it nearby.

Remove the chickpea mixture from the fridge, invert it onto a cutting board, and cut it into even rectangles, about ½ inch × 4 inches. Drop about one-third of the fries into the hot oil. Gently stir to prevent sticking, and cook until they are rich golden brown all over, 3 to 5 minutes. Use a slotted spoon to transfer the fries to the prepared baking sheet and immediately salt them. Repeat with the remaining fries, heating more oil as necessary between batches.

Serve the hot chickpea fries immediately, with the dip on the side. Store leftover fries in an airtight container in the fridge for up to 3 days. Store leftover dip in an airtight container in the fridge for up to 4 days.

VEGETARIAN MAINS

Lucy's Tacos Dorados de Papa

WITH AVOCADO SALSA

MAKES 12 TACOS

Both of my parents worked full-time (dad at the restaurant, mom pulling long nursing shifts), so my brother and I spent most of our days with our nanny, Lucy, who grew to be part of our family. Lucy nurtured my love of the kitchen and informed much of my understanding of food at a young age by letting me cook alongside her. But one of my favorite nights growing up was when my dad would make steak and mashed potatoes for dinner. Not necessarily because he made the best mash, but because I knew the next day, Lucy would make crispy potato tacos with the leftovers. Fried until golden and served with a spicy, creamy avocado salsa, this is my ode to those tacos. **VEG, GF**

MAKES 12 TACOS

SALSA

1 ripe Hass avocado
1 jalapeño, chopped into 1-inch pieces
1 large tomatillo, husked and rinsed well
Small handful of fresh cilantro leaves (about ¼ cup)
Juice of 1 lime, plus more as needed
2 tablespoons distilled white vinegar
Kosher salt

POTATO FILLING

1½ pounds russet potatoes, peeled and diced
Kosher salt
3 ounces queso fresco, crumbled
2 tablespoons chopped fresh cilantro
1 teaspoon ground cumin
Zest of 1 lime

12 (8-inch) corn tortillas
Neutral oil, for frying
Flaky sea salt
Sour cream and lime wedges, for serving (optional)

Make the salsa: In a blender, combine the avocado, jalapeño, tomatillo, cilantro, lime juice, vinegar, and salt to taste. Blend on high until smooth, 30 to 45 seconds. Adjust the consistency with more lime juice or a few tablespoons of water as needed.

Make the filling: Place the diced potatoes in a large pot and add cold water to cover and a generous pinch of salt. Bring to a simmer over medium heat and cook until fork-tender, about 25 minutes. Drain and let cool slightly, then transfer to a large bowl and use a fork to mash the potatoes. (I like to leave them a bit chunky, but the texture is up to you.) Add the queso fresco, cilantro, cumin, lime zest, and some salt and gently mix until combined. Taste and adjust the seasoning.

Warm 3 tortillas in a pan for about 15 seconds on each side, or wrap them in a damp paper towel and microwave them for 12 seconds.

Place the warmed tortillas on a work surface. Working with one at a time, spoon about ¼ cup of the filling in the middle, shaping it into a log so it reaches both edges of the tortilla. Tightly roll up the tortilla to enclose the filling and place it seam-side down on a plate. Cover the rolled tortilla with a damp paper towel so it won't dry out and crack as you roll the rest. Repeat with the remaining tortillas and filling.

In a cast-iron skillet, heat about 1 cup neutral oil over medium heat to between 330°F and 360°F. Using tongs, add 4 or 5 tacos to the hot oil, seam-side down. Cook for 2 to 3 minutes, then rotate them and cook for 2 to 3 minutes more to brown on all sides. Transfer to a paper towel–lined plate and season with salt. Repeat with the remaining tacos. Sprinkle with flaky salt and serve hot, with the salsa on the side and some sour cream and lime wedges, if desired.

Ricotta and Herb Crepes

WITH BALSAMIC ROASTED MUSHROOMS

MAKES 8 CREPES

In all of my restaurant jobs, I always volunteered for the task of creating vegetarian and vegan menus. To me, being able to get the most out of vegetables is the sign of a real cook—anyone can make a tasty ribeye. This recipe quickly became a favorite of mine when I was on veg duty. Admittedly, the crepes take some time and experience to get right, but once you get the technique down, it's a rather Zen practice. The crepes can be cooked, filled, and folded the day before, so these are great to have on hand to just pop in the oven for a reheat before serving. VEG

RICOTTA FILLING

2 cups whole-milk ricotta cheese, homemade (see page 154) or store-bought
Zest and juice of 1 lemon
1 tablespoon chopped fresh parsley
2 teaspoons chopped fresh thyme
Kosher salt and freshly ground black pepper

CREPES

1 cup whole milk
2 large eggs
2 tablespoons butter, melted
½ cup all-purpose flour
2 tablespoons finely chopped fresh parsley
1 tablespoon finely chopped fresh thyme
1 teaspoon garlic powder
1 teaspoon kosher salt

Make the filling: In a medium bowl, stir together the ricotta, lemon zest, lemon juice, parsley, and thyme. Season with a pinch of salt and pepper to taste. Cover and refrigerate while you prepare the crepes and mushrooms.

Make the crepes: In a large bowl, whisk together the milk, eggs, and melted butter until smooth, then sift the flour directly over the mixture and whisk well until smooth. Stir in the parsley, thyme, garlic powder, and salt. Cover and refrigerate for at least 30 minutes or up to overnight.

Meanwhile, make the mushrooms: Preheat the oven to 400°F. Line a baking sheet with aluminum foil.

In a large bowl, combine the mushrooms, vinegar, thyme, melted butter, olive oil, shallot, garlic, and some salt and pepper. Toss to coat, then spread the mushrooms evenly over the prepared baking sheet. Roast for 20 to 25 minutes, stirring halfway through the cooking time, until tender and golden.

Cook the crepes: Lightly grease an 8-inch nonstick skillet or crepe pan with butter or oil and heat over medium heat. Pour about ¼ cup of the crepe batter into the skillet and swirl the pan to coat the bottom evenly so there are no holes in the crepe. Cook until the edges just barely start to lift and the underside is a pale, even golden color, 1 to 2 minutes. Flip and cook for 30 seconds on the second side, then transfer the crepe to a plate or small baking dish and cover with a clean kitchen towel or foil. Repeat with the remaining batter; you should end up with 8 crepes.

Recipe and ingredients continue

MUSHROOMS

1 pound mixed mushrooms of your choice (I like oyster, cremini, and trumpets)
¼ cup balsamic vinegar
8 to 10 large thyme sprigs
2 tablespoons butter, melted
2 tablespoons olive oil
1 small shallot, thinly sliced into rings
2 garlic cloves, very thinly sliced
Kosher salt and freshly ground black pepper

Butter or oil, for greasing
Shaved Parmigiano-Reggiano cheese, for serving (optional)

Line another baking sheet with foil or parchment paper. Lay a crepe flat on your work surface and spoon about ¼ cup of the ricotta filling on one side of the crepe. Spread the filling evenly over half the crepe, then fold the exposed half of the crepe over to cover the ricotta. Fold the filled crepe into thirds so you're left with a triangle. Place the filled crepe on the prepared baking sheet and repeat with the remaining crepes and filling—it's okay if they overlap a bit on the pan. When the mushrooms are almost done, pop the crepes into the oven with them for 2 to 3 minutes, just enough to warm them through but not melt the ricotta too much.

Place the crepes on a serving platter or individual dinner plates, then top them with the hot roasted mushrooms. Finish with some freshly grated Parmigiano (if using) and dig in!

Tofu Katsu Lettuce Cups

WITH PICKLED RADISH AND SHICHIMI AÏOLI

SERVES 4 TO 6

I served this dish to a vegan neighbor a while back and it got a rave review. Since then, it's been a mainstay in my arsenal when cooking for vegan or vegetarian friends. If you're new to the wonders of shichimi togarashi, it's a wonderful Japanese seven-spice mix that can easily be found online or at a Japanese market. It packs a punch and definitely deserves a spot on your spice shelf. The crisp exterior and soft interior of the tofu create an interesting interplay of texture, while the sharp brine of the pickle and light spice of the shichimi aïoli give the dish those fun, vibrant finishes we love. VEG, V, DF

PICKLED RADISHES

1 bunch red radishes, cut into ⅛-inch-thick slices
2 teaspoons kosher salt
½ cup rice vinegar
2 tablespoons sugar
2 tablespoons mirin

SHICHIMI AÏOLI

½ cup vegan mayonnaise
1 tablespoon rice vinegar
2 teaspoons shichimi togarashi
Kosher salt

1 head Bibb or red-leaf lettuce, leaves separated (see Note)

TOFU KATSU

2 blocks extra-firm tofu
2 tablespoons ponzu
1 cup cornstarch
Kosher salt
2 cups panko breadcrumbs
About 4 cups neutral oil, for frying
1 tablespoon toasted sesame oil
Flaky sea salt
Shichimi togarashi

Make your own vegan aïoli—the recipe is on page 179!

Make the radishes: In a medium bowl, toss the radishes with 1 teaspoon of the salt. Let stand for 10 minutes.

Meanwhile, in a small saucepan, combine the vinegar, sugar, mirin, and remaining 1 teaspoon salt. Cook over medium heat, stirring occasionally, until the salt and sugar have dissolved and the mixture has come to a boil, 3 to 4 minutes. Remove from the heat and let cool slightly.

Rinse the radishes under cold water and pat dry with paper towels, then transfer to a clean jar or airtight container. Pour the vinegar mixture over the radishes, ensuring they are fully submerged (if they are not, they should be stirred once or twice as they cool to ensure even coating). Cover and refrigerate for at least 1 hour or up to 3 days before serving.

Make the aïoli: In a small bowl, stir together the mayonnaise, vinegar, and shichimi until combined. Season with salt to taste. Cover and refrigerate until ready to serve.

Arrange the lettuce leaves on a small platter, cover with a damp paper towel, and set aside in the fridge.

Make the tofu katsu: Cut each block of tofu in half lengthwise, then into 8 blocks of equal size, for a total of 16 pieces. Pat them dry well with paper towels. Place the blocks in a shallow dish and pour over the ponzu. Cover and marinate in the fridge for about 10 minutes.

In a medium bowl, whisk together ½ cup of the cornstarch, a pinch of salt, and ¾ cup cold water to combine. Place the panko in a separate shallow dish. Pat each

Recipe continues

NOTE: Use the large outer lettuce leaves to ensure the katsu will fit within them.

piece of tofu dry again, then dust all the pieces with the remaining ½ cup cornstarch, ensuring each piece is coated evenly. Working with one piece at a time, dunk the tofu into the cornstarch slurry to coat completely. Allow most of the slurry to drip off, then quickly dip the tofu into the panko, pressing gently on all sides to adhere well. Place the breaded tofu on a plate and repeat to coat the remaining tofu. (Stir the slurry between coatings, as cornstarch has a tendency to settle toward the bottom. If the slurry gets too thick, add a touch more water.)

Fill a large cast iron or other heavy duty skillet half way with the neutral oil (you may not need all 4 cups), then add the sesame oil and heat over medium heat to 350°F. Add half the tofu to the hot oil and cook until golden brown and crispy, 3 to 4 minutes per side. Transfer to a paper towel-lined plate to drain and sprinkle generously with flaky salt and shichimi. Repeat to fry the remaining tofu.

This dish is most fun served as a DIY situation: Arrange the fried tofu on a platter, then serve with the crispy lettuce, pickled radishes, and shichimi aïoli alongside for dolloping on top! Alternatively, preassemble all the lettuce wraps: Place a piece of tofu on 1 or 2 lettuce leaves, top with some radishes, dollop with aïoli, and serve. Leftover radishes and aïoli can be stored in separate airtight containers in the refrigerator for up to 1 week.

Vegan Shichimi Aïoli

MAKES ABOUT 2 CUPS

- 1 cup neutral oil (I like avocado oil for this)
- ¼ cup aquafaba (canned chickpea water)
- 1 tablespoon fresh lemon juice
- 2 teaspoons shichimi togarashi
- 2 teaspoons Dijon mustard
- 1 teaspoon kosher salt

In a 2-cup measuring cup, combine the oil, aquafaba, lemon juice, shichimi, mustard, and salt. Blend with an immersion blender on high speed until the mixture is thickened and the consistency of traditional aioli, about 45 seconds. Store the aïoli in a jar or airtight container in the refrigerator for up to 2 weeks.

Coconut-Peanut Braised Eggplant

SERVES 4

Eggplant can get a bad rap, but it's almost always user error, not the poor veggie's fault. Why? Eggplants are particularly porous vegetables and require some special prep attention to keep them from getting too oily or slimy. For the best results with this dish, use just enough oil so the eggplant can develop a good sear. Then the sponginess of the eggplant will work to your advantage as it absorbs a rich, gingery coconut braising liquid. The bright herbs at the end offer some lightness to contrast with the velvety braise, and crunchy peanuts create another textural element. Make some white rice and drizzle the dish with chili crisp for a perfect dinner. VEG, V, DF, GF

---

2 medium globe eggplants, stemmed and quartered lengthwise
Kosher salt
¼ cup neutral oil, plus more as needed
1 small red onion, thinly sliced
1 jalapeño, sliced into rings
2 (14-ounce) cans full-fat coconut milk
2 tablespoons grated fresh ginger
2 tablespoons vegan green curry paste
1 tablespoon smooth peanut butter
1 tablespoon vegan sambal oelek
¼ cup packed fresh cilantro leaves
¼ cup loosely packed fresh mint leaves
½ cup chopped salted roasted peanuts
Juice of 1 or 2 limes
Chili crisp, for serving
Cooked white rice, for serving

Place the eggplant quarters onto a plate and salt them generously. Let stand for 5 to 10 minutes to draw out some of the moisture, then pat them mostly dry with a paper towel.

In a large skillet, heat the oil over medium-high heat until it's very hot and rippling. Add half the eggplant quarters, cut-side down, and cook until browned nicely on the bottom, 2 to 3 minutes. Turn and cook on the second cut side until nicely browned, 2 to 3 minutes more. Transfer to a plate and repeat with the remaining eggplant quarters.

Add a bit more oil to the skillet as needed, then add the onion and jalapeño and cook over medium heat until they are barely softened and have become very fragrant, 4 to 5 minutes. Stir in the coconut milk, ginger, curry paste, peanut butter, sambal oelek, and a generous pinch of salt. Bring to a simmer, then return the seared eggplant quarters to the skillet and use a spoon to coat them with the sauce. Reduce the heat to medium-low and simmer, stirring every 5 minutes or so, until the eggplant is tender and fully cooked but not falling apart and mushy, 20 to 30 minutes. The sauce should be the consistency of buttermilk—thick enough to coat everything but not so thick that it's gloppy. If it gets too thick, add a touch of water to loosen it up.

Just before serving, sprinkle the cilantro, mint, and peanuts over the eggplant. Drizzle with the lime juice and some chili crisp, and serve with rice.

STAUB

Green Eggs in Purgatory

SERVES 2 TO 4

Shakshuka and eggs in purgatory have become ubiquitous on brunch menus for good reason, but I think they also deserve a place in your weekly dinner rotation. This dish is relatively easy to execute, and once you've got this technique down it's a great recipe to riff on with pantry staples or ingredients you have to use up, like greens that might be a bit wilted or wrinkly. The cooking of the eggs is an important step in this dish, and my biggest tip is to stop cooking them *just before* you think they're done. Make sure to serve it with some toasted bread for dipping! VEG, GF, DF

2 to 3 tablespoons olive oil
½ medium yellow onion, diced into ¼-inch pieces
1 jalapeño, chopped into ¼-inch pieces
3 garlic cloves, minced
1 bunch kale, leaves stemmed and chopped
1 medium leek, white and light green parts only, cut into ¼-inch-thick rings and washed well
3 or 4 scallions, white and green parts separated and thinly sliced
1 (15-ounce) can chickpeas, drained and rinsed
1 teaspoon ground cumin
1 teaspoon ground coriander
Kosher salt and freshly ground black pepper
1½ cups vegetable stock
6 large eggs
Flaky sea salt
Seeded Flatbreads (page 236), toasted sourdough bread, charred flour tortillas, or pita bread, for serving (optional)

Preheat the oven to 350°F.

In a large cast-iron skillet or other oven-safe pan, heat the olive oil over medium heat until it ripples. Add the onion and jalapeño and cook, stirring occasionally, until the edges of the onion have started to color and soften a bit, 4 to 5 minutes. Add the garlic and cook, stirring frequently, just until fragrant, another minute.

Stir in the kale, leek, and scallion whites and cook until the kale and leek are wilted and softened a bit, 4 to 5 minutes. Add the chickpeas, cumin, coriander, and a generous amount of kosher salt and pepper and stir well. Cook for 1 to 2 minutes to bloom the spices. Pour in the stock and bring to a simmer, then cook for a few minutes until the kale wilts a bit more. Taste and adjust the seasoning.

Reduce the heat to medium-low. Use a small spoon to push some of the mixture aside to create a little well, then crack an egg right into the well. Repeat with the remaining eggs. Place the pan in the oven and bake for 5 to 7 minutes, until the egg whites are set but the yolks are still runny (the eggs will continue to cook a bit after coming out of the oven). When the eggs are cooked to your liking, remove from the oven and sprinkle a bit of flaky salt on top of each egg.

Sprinkle the scallion greens over the dish and serve immediately, with bread for dipping.

Sesame Sweet Potato Potpie

SERVES 4 TO 6

If you're looking for a cozy vegetarian meal to whip up during the fall, you're in the right place. Sweet, salty, creamy, nutty—this potpie has got it all going on. Top it off with crisp puff pastry studded with toasted sesame seeds and you've got yourself a true textural delight. **VEG**

3 tablespoons butter
1 tablespoon toasted sesame oil
1 small to medium yellow onion, chopped into 1-inch pieces
3 small sweet potatoes (1½ to 2 pounds), peeled and diced into 1-inch cubes
6 ounces shiitake mushrooms, stemmed and quartered
1 bunch radishes, quartered lengthwise
3 garlic cloves, very thinly sliced
1 tablespoon minced fresh ginger
1½ tablespoons all-purpose flour
1½ cups vegetable stock
2 tablespoons white or light miso paste
2 tablespoons low-sodium soy sauce
Kosher salt and freshly ground black pepper
1 (10-ounce) bag frozen shelled edamame, thawed
2 or 3 scallions, thinly sliced on an angle
1 sheet frozen puff pastry, thawed per the package directions
1 large egg, beaten, for egg wash
2 to 3 tablespoons white sesame seeds
2 to 3 tablespoons black sesame seeds
Flaky sea salt

Preheat the oven to 400°F.

In a large cast-iron skillet or Dutch oven, melt the butter with the sesame oil over medium heat. Add the onion and cook until softened, translucent, and barely browning on the edges, about 5 minutes. Add the sweet potatoes, mushrooms, and radishes and cook, stirring occasionally, until the vegetables start to soften and begin to brown a bit, about 10 minutes. Add the garlic and ginger and cook for 1 to 2 minutes more just to cook out the raw garlic flavor, then stir in the flour and cook until it starts to turn golden, about 2 minutes more.

Gradually add the stock, stirring continuously to avoid lumps. Bring the mixture to a simmer, then stir in the miso and soy sauce, making sure to break up any lumps of miso. Simmer until the sweet potatoes are slightly tender on the outside but not falling apart and the sauce has thickened, 10 to 15 minutes. Taste and adjust the seasoning with kosher salt and pepper as needed. Remove from the heat, then stir in the edamame and scallions.

Transfer the sweet potato mixture to a 9 × 13-inch or large oval baking dish. Unfold the puff pastry and place it over the dish, doing your best to stretch it taut to avoid touching the hot mixture (this will help the pastry puff well). Press the pastry against the edges of the dish to seal it well, then brush the pastry with the egg wash. Sprinkle it evenly with white and black sesame seeds and a few big pinches of flaky salt.

Bake for 35 to 40 minutes, until the puff pastry is golden brown, puffed up, and super crisp all around. Allow the potpie to cool for at least 15 minutes or up to 25 minutes before scooping it into serving dishes and digging in!

To get clean lines with your sesame seeds, use two pieces of parchment paper set on a diagonal to cover up most of the puff pastry. Carefully sprinkle one color of sesame seeds to make a thick line, then move the parchment over, covering up the sesame seeds you just sprinkled and exposing a new piece of puff pastry. Use the opposite color sesame seeds to create another stripe, then repeat this process until the whole top is covered.

FISH & SEAFOOD MAINS

Spicy Fried Calamari and Zucchini

SERVES 2 TO 4

The fried calamari at my dad's brewery was always a top seller, and it was one of the first things I learned to make when I started working there. The squid here is delicately fried to maintain its tender bite while ensuring the outside is crisp as can be—this recipe is part fritto misto and part Seabright Brewery calamari. I serve this with a bright and spicy tomato dipping sauce, just like I did on my first day on the line at Seabright.

CALAMARI AND VEGETABLES

1 pound calamari tubes and tentacles
1 cup buttermilk
1 large egg
Kosher salt and freshly ground black pepper
1 small zucchini, sliced into ⅛-inch-thick discs
1 small lemon, sliced into ⅛-inch-thick discs and seeded
1 jalapeño, sliced into ⅛-inch-thick rings

SPICY TOMATO DIPPING SAUCE

3 tablespoons olive oil
1 pint cherry tomatoes
2 garlic cloves, very thinly sliced
1 teaspoon red pepper flakes
2 tablespoons red wine vinegar
Kosher salt

BREADING AND FRYING

6 cups neutral oil, for frying
1 cup all-purpose flour
1 cup cornstarch
1 tablespoon kosher salt
1 tablespoon lemon pepper seasoning

Make the calamari and vegetables: Rinse the calamari tubes and tentacles under cold water and pat dry with paper towels. Slice the tubes into rings about ½ inch thick.

In a large bowl, whisk together the buttermilk and egg. Season with kosher salt and black pepper, then add the calamari, zucchini, lemon, and jalapeño. Refrigerate for at least 15 minutes or up to overnight.

Meanwhile, make the sauce: In a medium saucepan, heat the olive oil over medium heat until it ripples. Add the tomatoes and cook until they start to blister and burst, 5 to 7 minutes. Add the garlic and red pepper flakes, and cook until the garlic is fragrant and slightly softened, 1 to 2 minutes more. Stir in the vinegar and cook until the vinegar has reduced by about half, 1 minute more. Taste and season with kosher salt; let cool to room temperature.

Bread and fry the calamari and vegetables: Preheat the oven to 275°F.

In a large heavy-bottomed pot or Dutch oven, heat the oil over medium-high heat to 375°F. Line a baking sheet with paper towels and set it nearby.

In a large bowl or deep baking dish, stir together the flour, cornstarch, kosher salt, lemon pepper seasoning, paprika, garlic powder, onion powder, and cayenne to combine.

Remove about one-third of the calamari and veggies from the buttermilk, letting the excess drip off, and place them in the flour mixture. Toss to coat, then transfer the coated calamari and veggies to a colander and shake off any excess flour. Using a slotted spoon or spider, carefully lower the coated calamari and veggies into the hot oil. Cook until golden brown and crispy all over, 3 to 4 minutes; if

Recipe and ingredients continue

2 teaspoons sweet paprika
1 teaspoon garlic powder
1 teaspoon onion powder
1 teaspoon cayenne pepper
Flaky sea salt

Lemon wedges, for serving

any pieces are sticking out of the oil, turn them after about 2 minutes to ensure they're evenly golden brown. (While the first batch fries, you can begin coating the next batch.) Use the slotted spoon or spider to transfer the fried calamari and veggies to the prepared baking sheet and immediately season with a hefty pinch of flaky salt. Keep warm in the oven while you cook the remaining calamari and veggies.

Arrange the fried calamari and zucchini on a serving platter or a baking sheet lined with clean paper towels or butcher paper. Serve with the dipping sauce and plenty of lemon wedges on the side for squeezing.

Quarter-Pound Fennel Crab Cakes

WITH OLD BAY SAUCE

MAKES 8 CRAB CAKES

I spend about three months out of every year working in the Hamptons, where the summer is filled with farmers' market jewels like juicy peaches and gorgeous tomatoes. Even so, the one thing I most look forward to cooking is the sweet, flaky blue crab. From pastas to salads, crab makes its way onto so many of my summer menus. My favorite is this luxe fennel crab cake with a sweet and herby filling that just screams summer in the Hamptons. When I'm on the West Coast, I reach for Dungeness crab. I usually serve one cake as a starter portion, or two if I am serving these as a main entree.

CRAB CAKES

2 tablespoons butter
1 small shallot, finely chopped
1 small fennel bulb, finely chopped (about ¼-inch pieces)
2 large eggs
½ cup mayonnaise
½ cup Italian breadcrumbs
2 tablespoons chopped mixed fresh herbs (I like dill, parsley, and fennel fronds)
1 tablespoon creamy prepared horseradish
1 tablespoon Dijon mustard
1 teaspoon dried dill
1 teaspoon garlic powder
Zest of 1 lemon
2 pounds lump blue or Dungeness crabmeat
Kosher salt and freshly ground black pepper
1½ cups panko breadcrumbs

Make the crab cakes: In a medium sauté pan, melt the butter over medium heat. Add the shallot and fennel and cook until softened and slightly translucent but not browned, 5 to 7 minutes. Remove from the heat and let cool completely, 5 to 10 minutes.

Line a baking sheet with parchment paper. In a large bowl, whisk together the shallot-fennel mixture, eggs, mayonnaise, breadcrumbs, herbs, horseradish, mustard, dill, garlic powder, and lemon zest to combine. Add 1 pound of the crabmeat, season with some salt and pepper, and mix thoroughly to combine. Add the remaining 1 pound crabmeat and gently fold it in just to combine. (The second addition of crab helps keep nice big chunks in the final product.) Shape the crab mixture into 8 equal-size patties and place them on the prepared baking sheet.

Place the panko in a shallow dish and season with salt and pepper. Gently coat each crab cake in the panko, pressing lightly to adhere, and shape them into pucks about 1½ inches thick. Place the coated crab cakes back on the baking sheet and refrigerate for at least 30 minutes or up to overnight.

Preheat the oven to 325°F. Line a baking sheet with aluminum foil or parchment.

Meanwhile, make the sauce: In a small bowl, whisk together the sour cream, mayonnaise, lemon juice, Old Bay, herbs, vinegar, and some salt. Taste and adjust the seasoning as needed.

Recipe and ingredients continue

OLD BAY SAUCE

½ cup sour cream
½ cup mayonnaise
Juice of 1 lemon
1 tablespoon Old Bay seasoning
1 tablespoon chopped mixed fresh herbs (same mix as you used for the crab cakes)
1 tablespoon white wine vinegar or apple cider vinegar
Kosher salt

1½ cups neutral oil, for frying
Lemon wedges, for serving

In a large sauté pan or cast-iron skillet, heat the oil over medium-high heat to between 325°F and 350°F (it should be hot but not smoking). Add half the crab cakes to the hot oil and cook until they're a deep, even golden brown color on both sides and heated through, 3 to 4 minutes per side. Transfer the cooked crab cakes to a plate and dab them with a paper towel to remove excess oil, then place them on the prepared baking sheet and pop them in the oven to keep them hot. Repeat with the remaining crab cakes.

To serve, arrange the hot crab cakes on a serving platter or individual plates, then top each with a dollop of the Old Bay sauce. Serve with any remaining sauce on the side and plenty of lemon wedges to squeeze over the top!

Whole Roasted Tamarind-Glazed Snapper

WITH SESAME-SCALLION SLAW

SERVES 2 TO 4

A whole roasted fish is a dramatic centerpiece for any dinner party. I like to use a white fish—in this case, red snapper—sturdy enough to stand up to the temperature of a high-heat roast as well as the full-bodied flavor of the sweet-tart tamarind glaze. DF, GF

TAMARIND GLAZE

¼ cup tamarind paste
Juice of 1 lime
2 tablespoons palm sugar or dark brown sugar
2 tablespoons rice vinegar
1 tablespoon grated fresh ginger
2 or 3 garlic cloves, grated or minced

SNAPPER

1 (2½- to 3-pound) whole red snapper, scaled and cleaned
1 lime, sliced into rounds
1 bunch scallions
Kosher salt

SESAME-SCALLION SLAW

1 bunch scallions, cut into 2-inch-long pieces, then sliced lengthwise into thin strips
2 tablespoons white sesame seeds, toasted
1 tablespoon neutral oil
1 tablespoon rice vinegar
1 teaspoon toasted sesame oil
Kosher salt

Lime wedges, for serving

Make the glaze: In a small bowl, whisk together the tamarind paste, lime juice, sugar, vinegar, ginger, and garlic until the sugar has dissolved and everything is well combined.

Make the snapper: Preheat the oven to 400°F. Line a baking sheet with aluminum foil.

Pat the fish dry with paper towels. Use a very sharp knife to make a few shallow slits running parallel from gill to belly on each side of the fish. Place the fish on the prepared baking sheet. Stuff the lime slices and scallions into the cavity of the fish.

Spoon about half the tamarind glaze generously over the entire surface of the snapper, ensuring both sides are well coated. Make sure to get the glaze into the slits you cut! Sprinkle the fish generously with salt. Roast for 15 minutes, then baste the fish with the remaining glaze and roast for 5 to 10 minutes more, until the fish flakes easily with a fork and reaches an internal temperature of 145°F.

Meanwhile, make the slaw: Place the scallions in a medium bowl with enough ice water to cover and soak for 5 minutes. Drain and dry them well. (This helps firm up the scallions and removes some of their harsh raw flavor.) Return the scallions to the bowl and add the sesame seeds, neutral oil, vinegar, sesame oil, and a pinch of salt. Mix well to coat the scallions. Refrigerate until ready to serve.

Remove the snapper from the oven and let it rest for a few minutes before carefully transferring it to a serving platter. Top the fish with some of the sesame-scallion slaw. Serve with the remaining slaw on the side and lime wedges for squeezing.

Baked Cod

WITH MUHAMMARA AND SUMAC ONIONS

SERVES 4

If you've never had muhammara, you're in for a treat! Originating in Syria, muhammara is usually served as a dip alongside warm pita bread, but I've found it's also a great sauce for anything from fish to steak. Here, it's served with flaky baked cod that's scented with a touch of cumin and lemon. On the side, a refreshing red onion and sumac salad cuts the creaminess of the muhammara and richness of the fish. The onion salad and muhammara can be made in advance, making this a great dinner party option, as all you need to do to finish the dish is pop the fish in the oven! (By the way, any leftovers make for great tacos.) DF

MUHAMMARA

1 (12-ounce) jar roasted red peppers, drained
¼ cup walnuts, toasted
¼ cup panko breadcrumbs
2 tablespoons pomegranate molasses
2 tablespoons olive oil
1 teaspoon ground cumin
1 teaspoon Aleppo pepper or sweet paprika
Juice of 1 lemon
Kosher salt

SUMAC ONIONS

½ small red onion, thinly sliced into half-moons
Small handful of fresh parsley leaves (about ¼ cup)
Zest and juice of ½ lemon
1 tablespoon ground sumac
1 teaspoon dried oregano
1 teaspoon kosher salt

COD

2 tablespoons olive oil
Zest and juice of ½ lemon
2 teaspoons ground cumin
4 (6- to 8-ounce) cod fillets
Kosher salt
Seeded Flatbreads (page 236), for serving (optional)

Preheat the oven to 375°F. Line a baking sheet with parchment paper or aluminum foil.

Make the muhammara: In a food processor or blender, combine the roasted peppers, walnuts, panko, molasses, olive oil, cumin, Aleppo pepper, and lemon juice. Blend on high speed until smooth and well combined, 1 to 2 minutes. Taste and adjust the seasoning with salt as needed.

Make the onions: Place the onions in a medium bowl. Add the parsley, lemon zest, lemon juice, sumac, oregano, and salt and toss to combine. Cover and marinate in the refrigerator while you cook the cod.

Make the cod: In a small bowl, whisk together the olive oil, lemon zest, lemon juice, and cumin. Lay the cod fillets on the prepared baking sheet, then drizzle with the oil mixture and rub it over the fillets so every surface is coated. Season each fillet with a hefty pinch of salt.

Bake the cod for 12 to 15 minutes, until the flesh is opaque and flakes easily with a fork and reaches an internal temperature of 145°F.

To serve, spoon a generous amount of the muhammara into the middle of a plate or large serving dish, then arrange the fish on top. Top with the marinated onions and serve immediately, with any remaining muhammara and onions alongside, and some seeded flatbreads, if you're feeling a little bit extra.

Lemongrass Mussels

WITH TOASTY BAGUETTE

SERVES 4 TO 6

This riff on the classic preparation of white wine-steamed mussels is a favorite of one of my clients, and for good reason. The gingery lemongrass broth is light enough to spotlight the brininess of the mussels without masking their delicate flavor, but hearty enough to stand up to the extra toasty bread (of which you will want plenty, to soak up all the tasty broth!).

MUSSELS

2 to 2½ pounds mussels (I like Green Lip or Prince Edward Island)
¼ cup neutral oil
1 (8-inch) lemongrass stalk
¼ cup fresh cilantro stems, cut into 1-inch pieces
1 tablespoon minced fresh ginger
2 or 3 garlic cloves, minced
1 Fresno chile, thinly sliced into rings
1 (14-ounce) can full-fat coconut milk
1 cup stock of your choice or water
2 tablespoons fish sauce
1 tablespoon light brown sugar
Kosher salt

TOASTY BAGUETTE

1 sourdough baguette, cut on a 45-degree angle into 1½-inch-thick slices
3 to 4 tablespoons butter, at room temperature
1 (1-inch) piece fresh ginger, peeled
Flaky sea salt

¼ cup chopped fresh cilantro leaves, for garnish
Lime wedges, for serving

Make the mussels: Place the mussels into a large bowl and add cold water to fill the bowl. Pick through the mussels and discard any that are cracked, open, or unwilling to shut after you squeeze them. Pick off any of the fuzz left on the mussels (this is known as the beard!). Drain the mussels, then return them to the bowl and refill with fresh cold water.

In a large pot or Dutch oven, heat the oil over medium heat until it ripples.

Use the back of a chef's knife to carefully but firmly whack the length of the lemongrass stalk. (This helps release the oils and maximize flavor output.) Cut the stalk into 1-inch pieces, then add the lemongrass to the pot and cook, stirring frequently, until very aromatic, about 2 minutes. Add the cilantro stems, ginger, garlic, and chile. Cook, stirring frequently, for 2 minutes more while you enjoy the aroma. Add the coconut milk, stock, fish sauce, and brown sugar. Bring the mixture to a light simmer, add some kosher salt, and check the seasoning. Simmer over medium to medium-low heat, stirring occasionally, for about 15 minutes to let the flavors meld.

Drain the mussels and add them to the pot. Stir well to coat. Cover and cook until all the mussels have popped open, 10 to 12 minutes. Discard any stubborn mussels that do not open.

Meanwhile, make the baguette: Spread both sides of the baguette pieces with the butter, then place them in a large cast-iron skillet or sauté pan. Toast over medium heat until deep golden brown on the bottom, about 4 minutes, then flip them over and toast on the other side until golden brown, about 4 minutes more. Rub both sides of each piece of bread with the ginger and sprinkle generously with flaky salt.

When the mussels are done, sprinkle them with the cilantro. Divide the mussels among bowls and spoon in plenty of the broth from the pot (avoiding any grit at the bottom). Serve with a few pieces of toasted baguette for dunking and lime wedges alongside for squeezing.

Broiled Sesame Salmon

WITH BROKEN GOCHUJANG TOFU SAUCE

SERVES 4 TO 6

I've always loved using the broiler to cook fish. It's quick, efficient, and cleaner than other methods. One catch: It requires a close eye, so don't scroll TikTok while this is in the oven! Another advantage to this particular dish is that you can prep the sauce in advance, which will let you keep all your attention on perfectly cooking the salmon. I like to serve the sauce either slightly cool or room temperature, which makes this dish an ideal option for a warm evening. DF

GOCHUJANG TOFU SAUCE

¼ cup gochujang
¼ cup rice vinegar
2 or 3 scallions, finely chopped
2 tablespoons low-sodium soy sauce
1 tablespoon toasted sesame oil
1 teaspoon grated fresh ginger
1 teaspoon sugar
½ (14-ounce) block silken tofu, drained

SALMON

1 tablespoon neutral oil, for greasing
1 (3-pound) salmon fillet (skin on or off)
2 tablespoons mayonnaise
1 teaspoon toasted sesame oil
2 tablespoons white sesame seeds
Kosher salt

Make the sauce: In a medium bowl, whisk together the gochujang, vinegar, scallions, soy sauce, sesame oil, ginger, sugar, and ¼ cup water until well combined. Use a paring knife to cut the tofu into small strips, then add the tofu to the sauce and stir very gently using a fork. You want decent-size chunks of the tofu to remain in the sauce (hence the "broken"), so take care not to overmix.

Make the salmon: Position racks in the center and lower third of the oven and preheat the broiler to high. Grease a high-sided baking dish with the neutral oil.

Cut ½-inch-deep slits every 2 inches along the entire flesh side of the fish. Place the fish in the prepared baking dish, skin-side down.

In a small bowl, whisk together the mayonnaise and sesame oil. Use a pastry brush to brush the mixture all over the fish, making sure to get it deep into the slits. Sprinkle with the sesame seeds and a generous pinch of salt, then broil for 8 to 10 minutes, until the salmon is pale pink all the way through and a rich golden brown on top. I take my salmon to an internal temperature of 128°F, but I technically have to tell you to take it to 145°F. Check the fish after 5 minutes to ensure the sesame seeds aren't burning; if they look too dark, move the fish down to the lower rack. Remove from the oven and let cool for at least 5 minutes, or up to 15 minutes.

Transfer the fish to a serving platter and spoon some of the sauce around it. Serve with the remaining sauce in a bowl on the side. Any leftover sauce can be stored in an airtight container in the fridge for up to 3 days.

Herby Buttered Scallops

WITH ARTICHOKES AND CRISPY CAPERS

SERVES 2 TO 4

Pan sauces are one of the first things you learn to make when learning how to cook meat in culinary school. You use the same pan in which you sear your protein to create a flavorful sauce by taking advantage of the Maillard reaction (Google it; it's science!) and flavored fat left behind in the pan. Quickly reducing the liquid and finishing with cold butter yields an intense, rich sauce. Once you've mastered this foundational technique, it's easily applied to chicken, beef, or in this case, sweet scallops and artichokes. **GF**

- 2 tablespoons olive oil, plus more as needed
- 3 tablespoons capers, drained, rinsed, and patted dry
- 1 pound large (8 to 12 count) diver scallops
- Kosher salt
- 1 small shallot, finely diced
- ¼ cup Champagne vinegar
- 1 cup dry white wine (I like Sancerre or Chablis)
- 1 cup chicken stock or vegetable stock
- 1 (12-ounce) can or jar artichoke hearts, drained and halved
- 2 tablespoons chopped fresh parsley, plus a small handful of fresh parsley leaves (about ¼ cup) for serving
- Zest and juice of 1 small lemon
- 6 tablespoons (¾ stick) butter, cut into small cubes and chilled
- Freshly ground black pepper

In a large cast-iron skillet or sauté pan, heat the olive oil over medium-high heat until it ripples. Add the capers and cook, stirring continuously, until crispy, 3 to 5 minutes. (Take care, as they may spatter as they fry!) Use a slotted spoon to transfer them to a paper towel–lined plate to drain. Reserve the oil.

Remove the "foot" (small side muscle) from the scallops if it's present, then pat them dry with paper towels and season with salt on both sides.

Return the skillet with the oil to medium-high heat. Heat until the pan just barely begins to smoke and the oil ripples. Add the scallops and cook until golden brown and caramelized on one side, 3 to 4 minutes. (These will finish cooking in the sauce, so don't overcook them now.) Transfer to a plate or rimmed baking dish, seared-side up.

Add a touch more oil to the skillet and reduce the heat to medium-low. Add the shallot and cook, stirring frequently, until softened and translucent, about 2 minutes. Pour in the vinegar and stir, scraping up any browned bits from the bottom of the pan. Remove from the heat and add the wine, then carefully return the pan to the stovetop. Simmer until reduced by half, 5 to 7 minutes. Stir in the stock and return the mixture to a simmer. Cook until reduced by about half, 7 to 10 minutes more.

Add the artichoke hearts to the pan and cook just until heated through, 1 to 2 minutes. Stir in the chopped parsley, lemon zest, and lemon juice, then reduce the heat to low. Whisk in the cold butter cubes, 2 or 3 at a time, until melted and incorporated into a creamy sauce. Return the scallops to the pan, seared-side up, and season with salt and pepper. Cook until they have turned from translucent to completely white on the inside, 1 to 2 minutes.

Arrange the scallops on a serving platter or divide them among individual plates, then top with the warm artichoke hearts. Spoon the sauce over the scallops and artichokes, then sprinkle with the capers and parsley leaves and serve.

Achiote-Marinated Shrimp and Pineapple Skewers

SERVES 4 TO 6

The iconic Mexican flavors of "al pastor" come together to flavor these shrimp and pineapple skewers. The intensely flavorful marinade, after a brief stint flavoring the shrimp, gets boiled to become a finishing glaze for the dish. Given the amount of acid from the pineapple and the lime, be sure not to let the shrimp marinate too long or they'll get mushy on you. I like to pierce the shrimp at two points: through the tail first, then again at the head, so they stay flat and cook evenly. Remember, if you're using bamboo skewers, you'll want to give them a soak for a few hours! This goes great with Tomatillo Arroz Verde (page 127) and some charred corn tortillas. DF, GF

3 dried guajillo chiles, stemmed, seeded, and cut into 2-inch pieces
5 garlic cloves, peeled
1 teaspoon whole black peppercorns
5 or 6 whole cloves
1 cup pineapple juice
Juice of 2 limes
1 tablespoon achiote paste
1 tablespoon neutral oil
1 teaspoon dried oregano
Kosher salt
1½ pounds large (16 to 20 count) shrimp, peeled and deveined
½ pineapple, peeled and cut into 1-inch pieces
¼ cup chopped fresh cilantro
Nonstick cooking spray
Flaky sea salt
Lime wedges, for serving

Open up a window or turn the exhaust fan on (the fumes from the chiles can be strong!). Place the chiles, garlic, peppercorns, and cloves in a cold large sauté pan or cast-iron skillet. Cook over medium-high heat, stirring frequently as the pan heats up and everything begins to toast, until the mixture is very fragrant and the chiles have begun to turn light brown, 6 to 8 minutes. Immediately remove from the heat and transfer the mixture into a blender. Add the pineapple juice, lime juice, achiote paste, oil, oregano, and a good pinch of kosher salt. Blend on high speed until the marinade is super smooth, 1 to 2 minutes.

In a large bowl, combine the shrimp and the achiote marinade and stir well to coat the shrimp. Let the shrimp marinate for at least 30 minutes or up to 2 hours in the fridge.

Heat a grill to medium-high.

Thread the shrimp and pineapple onto skewers, alternating them until each skewer is full—usually 3 or 4 shrimp and 2 or 3 pineapple pieces per skewer. You'll have 8 to 10 skewers total.

Pour the leftover marinade from the shrimp into a medium pot and bring to a simmer over medium heat. Cook, stirring frequently, for about 10 minutes, until sauce turns a deep red color, then remove from the heat and stir in the cilantro.

Coat each skewer with a touch of cooking spray, then grill until the shrimp are opaque white all the way through, 2 to 3 minutes on each side. You want some good charring on both sides, but don't overcook the shrimp.

Place the skewers onto a serving platter and spoon over a bit of the marinade. Finish with a sprinkling of flaky salt and serve with lime wedges alongside for squeezing.

Chicharrón-Crusted Halibut

WITH SWEET CORN SUCCOTASH

SERVES 4

The first time I cooked this dish, I did it with scallops. While I loved the combo of the sweet corn and scallop with chicharrónes (fried pork rinds), in the end I decided the dish needed a hearty fish like halibut to hit all the notes I was looking for. Halibut can be a notoriously difficult piece of fish to cook, as its lean nature and dense structure tend to cause it to dry out quickly, but the little bit of spiced mayo and chicharrón crust ensure a nice moist fillet every time. **DF, GF**

HALIBUT

Nonstick cooking spray
¼ cup mayonnaise
Zest and juice of ½ lime
1 teaspoon chili powder
4 (6- to 8-ounce) halibut fillets
Kosher salt
½ cup finely crumbled chicharrones (fried pork rinds)

SUCCOTASH

2 tablespoons olive oil
Kernels from 1 ear sweet yellow corn (about 1 cup)
1 small green zucchini, cut into ½-inch cubes
1 red bell pepper, cut into ½-inch pieces
1 large shallot, sliced into rings
1 jalapeño, finely diced
¼ cup chopped fresh cilantro, plus some whole leaves for garnish
Kosher salt
Lime wedges, for serving

Make the halibut: Preheat the oven to 400°F. Line a baking sheet with parchment paper or aluminum foil, then coat it with cooking spray.

In a small bowl, stir together the mayonnaise, lime zest, lime juice, and chili powder until well combined.

Pat the halibut fillets dry with paper towels, then place them on the prepared baking sheet and season with salt. Spread the mayonnaise mixture evenly over the top of each fillet. Press the chicharrones onto the mayonnaise mixture to form a crust.

Bake for 12 to 15 minutes, until the fish is cooked through and the chicharrón crust is golden brown. You'll know the halibut is done when the fish is firm all the way through and opaque juices have just begun to run; a thermometer should read 132°F.

Meanwhile, make the succotash: In a large sauté pan, heat the olive oil over medium-high heat until it ripples. Add the corn kernels, zucchini, bell pepper, shallot, and jalapeño. Cook, stirring frequently, until the vegetables are bright, fragrant, and cooked through but still have a bit of a bite to them, 5 to 7 minutes. Stir in the cilantro.

Just before serving, season the succotash with salt and add cilantro leaves for garnish. Serve the halibut and succotash on individual plates or a large platter. Either way, squeeze a generous amount of lime juice over the fish and succotash just before diving in and serve with additional lime wedges on the side.

MEAT & POULTRY MAINS

Spice Mix

MAKES ABOUT ¼ CUP

2 teaspoons kosher salt
1 teaspoon garlic powder
1 teaspoon onion powder
1 teaspoon sweet paprika
1 teaspoon dried thyme
1 teaspoon brown sugar
½ teaspoon cayenne pepper
½ teaspoon ground cinnamon
½ teaspoon ground allspice
½ teaspoon red pepper flakes
½ teaspoon freshly ground black pepper
½ teaspoon ground cumin

In a small bowl, stir together the salt, garlic powder, onion powder, paprika, thyme, brown sugar, cayenne, cinnamon, allspice, red pepper flakes, black pepper, and cumin until combined.

Mango-Coconut Braised Chicken

SERVES 4

During the COVID-19 lockdown, like everyone else, I searched for ways to stay engaged with friends. Cooking together over Zoom let us catch up without actually being at the dinner table. Early in the week, I'd send my pals the shopping list, then on the weekend I walked us through the recipe. This chicken hit all the right comfort-food notes—rich, (not too) sweet, smoky, a little punch of heat—and quickly became a favorite. Ryan and I still make it! The spice mix is so delish, I always double it to keep extra on hand. It will keep in an airtight container at room temperature for up to two weeks, and—little extra tip—it's incredible on popcorn. **DF**

- 4 to 6 bone-in, skin-on chicken thighs (1 to 1½ pounds total)
- 3 tablespoons neutral oil
- Spice mix (recipe at left)
- 1 teaspoon toasted sesame oil
- 1 small yellow or red onion, chopped into 1-inch pieces
- 1 red bell pepper, chopped into 1-inch pieces
- 1 jalapeño, minced
- 1 garlic clove, minced
- 1 (1-inch) piece fresh ginger, peeled and finely chopped
- 1 (14-ounce) can full-fat coconut milk
- 1 tablespoon low-sodium soy sauce
- 1 teaspoon Worcestershire sauce
- 1 head broccoli, cut into florets
- 1 large ripe mango, pitted, peeled, and cut into large chunks
- Kosher salt
- 1 lime, halved
- 2 tablespoons chopped fresh cilantro

Pat the chicken thighs dry with a paper towel, then coat them with all of the seasoning mix.

Heat a large, straight-sided pan or cast-iron skillet over medium-high heat for 2 to 3 minutes. Add 2 tablespoons of the neutral oil and the sesame oil and heat until the oils ripple. Add the chicken and cook for 3 to 4 minutes on each side. You want good caramelization on both sides, so don't be afraid if you see some very dark browning, or even blackening! Transfer the chicken to a plate.

Add the remaining 1 tablespoon neutral oil to the pan (no need to wipe it out), then add the onion, bell pepper, jalapeño, garlic, and ginger. Cook over medium-high heat, stirring frequently, until super fragrant, about 2 minutes. Add the coconut milk, soy sauce, and Worcestershire. Bring to a boil, then reduce the heat to medium-low. Stir in the broccoli and mango, along with a hefty pinch of kosher salt, then return the seared chicken to the pan along with any juices on the plate. Simmer the chicken until cooked all the way through and the center has no pink near the bone when cut into, 20 to 30 minutes, flipping it halfway through.

Just before serving, squeeze the juice from the lime halves over the chicken and sprinkle with the cilantro.

Tinga Turkey Meatballs and Cabbage Slaw

SERVES 4 TO 6

The chef at my dad's brewery went through *quite* a phase—as many chefs and restaurants were wont to do in the early aughts—of putting chipotle in just about everything on the menu. From barbecue sauce, to soups, to Bloody Marys—it was everywhere and admittedly it turned me off from the tart, smoky pepper. Now, the early 2000s are back, and I have fallen in love with the chipotle pepper. They're a great option for adding deep umami and spice to dishes like this version of Mexican tinga. This recipe draws on the flavors and presentation of the classic dish, which is usually made from shredded chicken in a light tomato and onion sauce, but I swapped the chicken for ground turkey and rolled it into meatballs, stewing them down in a rich tomato sauce. **GF**

MEATBALLS

Nonstick cooking spray
1½ pounds ground turkey
½ cup pulverized corn tortilla chips or tostadas
¼ cup finely chopped fresh cilantro
1 large egg
1 large egg yolk
1 canned chipotle pepper in adobo sauce, chopped
1 tablespoon dark chili powder
2 teaspoons kosher salt
1½ teaspoons garlic powder
1½ teaspoons onion powder

SAUCE

2 tablespoons neutral oil
1 small white onion, sliced into ¼-inch-thick half-moons
2 garlic cloves, sliced
3 Roma (plum) tomatoes, chopped into 1-inch pieces
2 to 4 canned chipotle peppers in adobo sauce, chopped
1 (14-ounce) can tomato puree
2 teaspoons garlic powder
1 teaspoon dried Mexican oregano
Kosher salt

Make the meatballs: Preheat the oven to 425°F. Line two baking sheets with aluminum foil, then coat them with cooking spray.

In a large bowl, combine the turkey, tortilla chips, cilantro, egg, egg yolk, chipotle, chili powder, salt, garlic powder, and onion powder. Mix with your hands or a sturdy spoon until thoroughly combined.

Use a cookie scoop or two spoons to form the mixture into meatballs about 1 inch in diameter, placing them on the prepared baking sheets and spacing them evenly apart. You should have 25 to 30 meatballs. Coat the meatballs with a bit more cooking spray, then bake for 12 to 15 minutes, until they are cooked through, are no longer pink on the inside, and have begun to brown slightly.

Meanwhile, make the sauce: In a large heavy-duty pot or Dutch oven, heat the neutral oil over medium heat until it ripples. Add the onion and cook until softened and slightly translucent but not brown, 5 to 6 minutes. Add the garlic and cook until fragrant, 1 to 2 minutes more, then stir in the chopped tomatoes and chipotles. Cook until the tomatoes start to break down and release some of their liquid, about 5 minutes.

Add the tomato puree, garlic powder, oregano, and salt to taste.

Recipe and ingredients continue

Feeling a little bit EXTRA?
Fry your own tostadas—instructions are on the next page!

SLAW
¼ head green cabbage, shaved
¼ cup chopped fresh cilantro
2 tablespoons olive oil
Zest and juice of 1 lime
Kosher salt

FOR SERVING
8 to 12 yellow corn tostadas
1 cup Mexican crema
Lime wedges

Bring to a simmer. Add the cooked meatballs along with any drippings from the baking sheets. Cook, stirring occasionally, until the sauce thickens slightly and the meatballs have soaked up plenty of flavor from the sauce, 25 to 30 minutes.

Meanwhile, make the slaw: In a large bowl, combine the cabbage, cilantro, olive oil, lime zest, and lime juice. Sprinkle with some salt and toss well to coat evenly.

To serve, slather a tostada with a tablespoon or two of crema, then arrange a few meatballs on top, spooning over some of the sauce and onions as well. Top with a hefty pile of slaw, and serve with lime wedges alongside for squeezing.

Chili-Dusted Tostadas

MAKES 8 TO 12

½ to 1 cup neutral oil
8 to 12 (8-inch) corn tortillas
1 to 2 tablespoons chili powder
Kosher salt

Line a plate or baking sheet with paper towels. In a medium sauté pan or cast-iron skillet, heat ½ cup of the oil over medium heat for about 3 minutes, then drop a tortilla into the oil. It should release small, consistent bubbles right as it hits the oil. Use a spoon to push the edges and center of the tortilla down to ensure it stays relatively flat. Cook until the first side is a nice golden brown color, about 3 minutes, then flip the tortilla and cook until golden brown and crisp all over, 2 to 3 minutes more. Transfer to the paper towel–lined plate or baking sheet to drain and immediately sprinkle with a good dusting of chili powder and a generous pinch of salt. Repeat with the remaining tortillas, adding more oil as needed to ensure there is at least ¼ inch in the pan and letting it get hot between batches. The tostadas can be stored in a zip-top bag or airtight container at room temperature for a day or two.

Chinese Black Bean Braised Short Ribs and Chive Buttered Turnips

SERVES 4 TO 6

A good short rib recipe is a *must* for any home cook's or chef's recipe repertoire. While the dish takes some time to slowly braise into unctuous, fall-apart chunks of beef, I promise the wait is well worth it. We're calling on the umami bomb that is Chinese black bean paste here (rather than the often-used tomato paste) and bolstering those flavors with plenty of ginger and soy sauce for a rich, Chinese-influenced version of a classic braised shortie.

SHORT RIBS

2 tablespoons neutral oil
4 pounds bone-in beef short ribs
2 teaspoons freshly ground white pepper
Kosher salt
1 small yellow onion, thinly sliced into half-moons
4 garlic cloves, smashed and peeled
1 (3-inch) piece fresh ginger, thinly sliced into matchsticks
½ cup Chinese black bean garlic sauce
2 tablespoons low-sodium soy sauce
1 tablespoon sugar
3 cups beef stock

CHIVE BUTTERED TURNIPS

2 bunches Tokyo turnips or baby turnips, cut in half
1 cup beef stock
3 garlic cloves, smashed and peeled
3 tablespoons butter
1 teaspoon sugar
Kosher salt
2 tablespoons minced fresh chives, plus more for serving (optional)

1 tablespoon cornstarch

Make the short ribs: Preheat the oven to 275°F.

In a large Dutch oven or other heavy-bottomed pot with a lid, heat the neutral oil over medium-high heat until it ripples. Season the short ribs with the white pepper and a generous pinch of salt on all sides. Working in batches, add the short ribs to the pot and cook until browned on all sides, 3 to 4 minutes per side, then transfer to a plate. Repeat to brown the remaining short ribs. Discard most of the fat from the pot, leaving only a tablespoon or two behind.

Add the onion, garlic, and ginger to the fat in the pot and cook over medium heat until fragrant, 2 to 3 minutes. Add the black bean garlic sauce, soy sauce, and sugar. Stir and cook for 1 to 2 minutes more, just to coat the aromatics well, then pour in the stock and stir, scraping up any browned bits from the bottom of the pot. Return the short ribs to the pot, cover, and transfer to the oven. Braise for 3 for 4 hours, until the short ribs are tender and the meat is falling off the bones.

Make the turnips: Twenty-five minutes before the short ribs are done, combine the turnips, stock, garlic, 2 tablespoons of the butter, the sugar, and a good pinch of salt in a medium pot. Bring to a simmer over medium heat and cook until the turnips are tender all the way through but not mushy and the liquid has reduced to a glaze, 15 to 20 minutes. Remove

Recipe continues

NOTE: If you want a thicker sauce, make more cornstarch slurry and stir it in. Cornstarch must be mixed with water before it's added to the sauce or it will clump. The slurry needs to cook at a gentle boil for at least 1 minute to fully activate and cook out the raw taste, so ensure you've cooked the sauce long enough to activate and thicken before adding more slurry!

from the heat and stir in the chives, remaining 1 tablespoon butter, and salt to taste. Cover to keep warm.

Transfer the short ribs to a serving dish or rimmed baking sheet and cover with aluminum foil. Strain the braising liquid through a fine-mesh sieve or colander into a separate saucepan, and reserve all the onion-bean mixture. Skim off excess fat from the braising liquid with a spoon or ladle, then bring the liquid to a simmer over medium heat.

In a small bowl, mix the cornstarch with about 1 tablespoon water to create a slurry. Whisk the slurry into the simmering liquid and cook for a minute or two until it has thickened to the consistency of a sauce (see Note). Fold the reserved onion-bean mixture into the sauce and cook until it is warmed through.

Plate the braised short ribs alongside the chive buttered turnips. Drizzle the sauce over the ribs and garnish with chives, if desired.

Peach Mostarda Grilled Pork Chops

SERVES 6

Summer is for two things: grilling and peaches. With that, I am pleased to introduce you to the ultimate pork chop, which incorporates both. The concept of pairing pork with fruit is nothing new, but every time I make this recipe I'm reminded of just how effective it is. The mostarda is tart and sweet with just enough zip from the mustard, making it a perfect foil for the juicy grilled chops. I like to serve it at room temperature, but it's delicious served slightly chilled as well; it keeps in an airtight container in the fridge for up to a week. Time permitting, I always recommend brining pork chops for maximum juiciness (recipe follows). If you lost track of time on a long summer afternoon, go ahead and skip the brine—you'll still love these chops. **DF, GF**

MOSTARDA

1 tablespoon olive oil
1 small shallot, minced
1 teaspoon grated fresh ginger
1 Fresno chile or jalapeño, minced
3 ripe peaches, pitted and cut into 1-inch pieces
¼ cup loosely packed light brown sugar
¼ cup apple cider vinegar
2 tablespoons whole-grain mustard
½ teaspoon curry powder
Kosher salt and freshly ground black pepper

PORK CHOPS

6 (8-ounce) bone-in pork chops, 1½ inches thick
2 tablespoons apple cider vinegar
Olive oil
Kosher salt and freshly ground black pepper

Make the mostarda: In a medium pot, heat the olive oil over medium heat until it ripples. Add the shallot, ginger, and chile and cook, stirring frequently, until the mixture is very fragrant and the shallot looks translucent, 2 to 3 minutes. Add the peaches, brown sugar, vinegar, and 2 tablespoons water. Reduce the heat to medium-low and cook, stirring every few minutes, until the liquid reduces, becomes syrupy and glossy, and looks like loose jam or marmalade, 8 to 10 minutes. Remove from the heat and fold in the mustard, curry powder, and salt and pepper to taste. Cover until you're ready to eat.

Make the chops: Preheat a grill to medium-high for 10 to 15 minutes.

Pat the chops dry with paper towels on both sides, then rub them with the vinegar and some olive oil. Season with salt and pepper, then throw them on the grill and cook until they reach 145°F, about 6 minutes on each side (my preferred temperature is 134°F).

Transfer the chops to a plate, loosely tent with aluminum foil, and let rest for at least 10 minutes or up to 20 minutes before slicing. Serve the chops with a generous dollop of the mostarda.

Let's brine these chops! While it does require a bit of foresight, brining the chops for a few hours helps keep them super juicy and adds a great layer of flavor to the meat itself. Instructions are on page 220.

Apple Cider Brine

MAKES ENOUGH FOR 4 TO 6 PORK CHOPS

½ cup apple cider vinegar
¼ cup lightly packed dark brown sugar
2 tablespoons kosher salt
1 tablespoon whole black peppercorns
10 thyme sprigs, or 2 teaspoons dried thyme

In a small pot, combine the vinegar, brown sugar, salt, peppercorns, and thyme. Bring to a boil over high heat, stirring until the salt and sugar have dissolved. Remove from the heat and let cool to room temperature, 20 to 30 minutes.

In a large bowl, combine 3 cups cold water and 3 heaping cups of ice, then add the vinegar mixture. Nestle the pork chops in the brine and refrigerate for at least 2 hours or up to 8 hours. Drain the chops and pat them completely dry with paper towels before seasoning and grilling as directed.

Grilled Tri-Tip

WITH GUAJILLO PEANUT SALSA AND CUCUMBER ONION SALAD

SERVES 2 TO 4

The flavors and techniques of Mexican cooking have heavily influenced the way I cook, and the cuisine's sauce-making has always fascinated me the most. I learned this salsa from a family friend who used chile de árbol in place of the guajillo chiles for a super-spicy accompaniment to anything from eggs to carne asada. Here, we serve it alongside grilled tri-tip steak doused in a light beer marinade and a quick cucumber and onion salad that balances the richness of the steak and smoky spice of the salsa. DF

STEAK

1½ to 2 pounds tri-tip steak
1 cup light beer, such as Corona (whatever's left in the bottle is for you!)
2 tablespoons neutral oil
¼ medium white onion, grated on a box grater
Zest of 1 lime
1 teaspoon ground cumin
Kosher salt

SALSA

¾ cup neutral oil
¼ medium white onion, chopped into 1-inch pieces
2 garlic cloves, smashed and peeled
5 large dried guajillo chiles, stemmed, seeded, and torn into 1- to 2-inch pieces
½ cup raw unsalted peanuts
¼ cup packed fresh cilantro
¼ cup distilled white vinegar
2 teaspoons sugar or honey
Kosher salt

Make the steak: In a large bowl or resealable bag, combine the steak, beer, neutral oil, onion, lime zest, cumin, and some salt. Mix to ensure the steaks are evenly coated, then cover the bowl or seal the bag and marinate in the refrigerator for at least 1 hour or ideally 4 hours.

Make the salsa: Meanwhile, in a heavy-duty medium skillet or cast-iron pan, combine the neutral oil, onion, and garlic and cook over medium heat until the onion is translucent and garlic is just barely light golden, 5 to 7 minutes. Add the chiles and cook, stirring frequently, until the chiles have softened and turned a deep reddish brown. (The chiles will give off a strong aroma, so turn on that fan!) Add the peanuts and cook until they are lightly toasted, 1 to 2 minutes more. Remove from the heat and let cool to room temperature, 5 to 10 minutes, then transfer the mixture to a blender or food processor. Add the cilantro, vinegar, sugar, and salt to taste. Pulse in quick bursts until the mixture is broken down to a fairly fine salsa—it should almost resemble chili crisp. Take care not to puree the mixture until smooth. The oil may separate, but that's fine—just stir it up before serving.

Make the salad: In a large bowl, combine the onion and cucumber. Add lemon juice, Tajín, and some salt and pepper. Toss gently to coat. Refrigerate until ready to serve.

Preheat a grill to medium-high for 10 to 15 minutes.

Remove the steak from the marinade and shake off any excess. Grill for

Recipe and ingredients continue

SALAD

½ medium white onion, sliced into ⅛-inch-thick half-moons
1 English cucumber, sliced on an angle into ⅛-inch-thick half-moons (see Note)
Juice of 1 lemon
1 tablespoon Tajín seasoning
Kosher salt and freshly ground black pepper
Flaky sea salt

Warm corn tortillas, for serving (optional)

8 to 10 minutes per side, until desired doneness is reached: For rare, aim for an internal temp of 118°F; for medium-rare, aim for 122°F to 124°F; and for medium, wait for 128°F to 130°F. Transfer the steak to a plate or cutting board and let rest for at least 10 minutes, or up to 20 minutes, before slicing.

To serve, slice the steak against the grain into thin strips, then arrange on dinner plates or a serving platter. Drizzle the salsa over the top, sprinkle with flaky salt, then mound the cucumber salad next to the steak. Serve with warm corn tortillas, if desired, and any remaining salsa on the side. Leftover salsa can be stored in an airtight container in the refrigerator for up to 2 weeks.

NOTE: For visual appeal, use a vegetable peeler to remove some of the skin from the cucumber before slicing, if you like.

Pork Milanese

WITH APPLE, FENNEL, AND RADISH SALAD

SERVES 4

Milanese, katsu, schnitzel—while they all may be slightly different, they're equally delicious for their crisp exterior and juicy, meaty interior. One thing is for certain when serving a fried dish like this: you'll need a bright, herby, and refreshing side with it to cut the richness. Here, we reach for spicy radish, herby fennel, and sweet, tart apple finished in a mustardy dressing—a classic pairing for pork. While I like the look of long French radishes, the conventional variety work just fine here too.

MILANESE

4 (4-ounce) boneless pork chops
1 teaspoon garlic powder
1 teaspoon onion powder
Kosher salt and freshly ground black pepper
1 cup all-purpose flour
2 large eggs
1 cup panko breadcrumbs
1 cup Italian breadcrumbs

SALAD

1 bunch French breakfast radishes (6 to 8), quartered lengthwise
1 small Granny Smith apple, cored and cut into ¼-inch matchsticks
1 medium fennel bulb, shaved on a mandoline or by hand, plus 2 tablespoons coarsely chopped fennel fronds
¼ cup 1-inch-long sliced fresh chives
2 tablespoons apple cider vinegar
2 tablespoons olive oil
1 tablespoon whole-grain mustard
Kosher salt and freshly ground black pepper

About 2 cups neutral oil, for frying
Flaky sea salt

Make the Milanese: Lay a sheet of plastic wrap on a work surface, then place the chops on top. Season them on both sides with the garlic powder, onion powder, kosher salt, and pepper. Cover the chops with another sheet of plastic wrap and use a meat mallet to tenderize and flatten them to about half their original thickness (use some force!). You may need to flip them over to pound both sides for an even shape.

Place the flour in a shallow dish. In another shallow dish, whisk the eggs with 2 tablespoons water. In a third shallow dish, combine the panko and Italian breadcrumbs and season well with kosher salt and pepper.

Dredge each pork chop in the flour, shaking off any excess. Dip in the beaten eggs, allowing any excess to drip off, then press into the breadcrumb mixture, coating both sides evenly. Place breaded pork chops on a plate or baking sheet, then repeat with the remaining chops. Refrigerate while you make the salad or for up to 4 hours.

Make the salad: In a large bowl, combine the radishes, apple, shaved fennel, fennel fronds, and chives.

In a small bowl, whisk together the vinegar, olive oil, mustard, and some kosher salt and pepper. Pour the dressing over the salad and toss gently to coat. Cover and refrigerate until ready to serve.

In a large skillet or cast-iron pan, heat the neutral oil over medium-high heat to about 360°F. Working in batches as needed, cook the pork chops until golden brown and cooked through (no longer pink on the inside), 3 to 4 minutes per side. Transfer to a paper towel–lined plate to drain and immediately season with flaky salt. (If you're working in batches, you can keep them hot in a 300°F oven.)

Divide the pork chops among four plates. Serve each with a generous helping of the salad spilling off the side.

Roasted Chicken

WITH "UNDER THE CHICKEN" ONION CHUTNEY

SERVES 4

I don't think we as parents (read: cooks) are supposed to pick a favorite child (read: recipe), but I will say boldly this is my favorite in this book. It requires little foresight and minimal ingredients. You will need to spatchcock the chicken, which provides optimal surface area for crisping the skin, and quicker cooking—but you can buy a chicken prepared this way or ask your butcher to do it. But the star of this show is the lemony onion chutney that comes together from the roasted aromatics and chicken drippings. It has a rich, umami flavor, a hint of bitterness and tang, and a luxurious finish. **DF, GF**

---

1 large lemon, sliced into ¼-inch-thick rounds and seeded
1 small sweet onion, sliced into ¼-inch-thick rings
1 bunch scallions, white and green parts separated
4 garlic cloves, peeled
½ cup olive oil, plus more as needed
1 (4½-pound) whole chicken
2 teaspoons garlic powder
1 teaspoon dried thyme
1 teaspoon freshly ground black pepper, plus more as needed
Kosher salt

NOTE: Cooking times and oven temperatures vary, so adjust the oven temperature or rack position as you roast. Start checking the chicken and veggies after about 25 minutes.

Preheat the oven to 415°F. Line a rimmed baking sheet with aluminum foil or parchment paper.

Arrange the lemon, onion, scallion whites, and garlic evenly on the baking sheet and drizzle them with ¼ cup of the olive oil. Spatchcock the chicken by removing the spine, then pat the chicken dry with a paper towel. Place the chicken on top of the lemon and onion, then drizzle with the remaining ¼ cup oil and rub it all over the chicken. Evenly sprinkle the chicken with the garlic powder, thyme, pepper, and a generous amount of salt (at least 1 tablespoon).

Roast for 40 to 50 minutes (see Note), until the chicken reaches 165°F (use an oven-safe probe thermometer inserted into the breast), the skin is a deep, rich golden brown and perfectly crisp, and the lemon-onion mix is soft and caramelized (even borderline charred in some parts, that's okay!). Remove from the oven and let stand for 10 minutes, undisturbed.

Meanwhile, thinly slice the scallion greens and place them in a small bowl. Cover with a damp paper towel or plastic wrap.

Transfer the roasted chicken to a clean baking sheet or a large plate. Scoop the onion-lemon mixture onto a cutting board and finely chop it—think the consistency of a chunky tapenade. Add the lemon-onion mixture to the bowl with the scallion greens, then add all the chicken drippings and fat from the baking sheet and mix well. Taste and adjust the seasoning with salt and pepper as needed. You may also want to add a touch more olive oil to give it a saucier consistency.

Carve the chicken however you please and serve with the onion chutney alongside.

Lemongrass Lamb Kebabs

WITH SWEET FISH SAUCE GLAZE

SERVES 4 TO 6

If I had to summarize this dish in one word it would be *drama*! From the bold presentation of the kebabs grilled on the stalks of lemongrass to the intense nuóc chấm–inspired glaze, this dish is all about intense, funky, fun flavors. If you've never had nuóc chấm before, prepare for your new fav condiment. It's a classic punch Vietnamese dipping sauce that's a combo of fish sauce, lime juice, and a bit of sugar to round it all out. I love to serve this with some short-grain white rice and undressed shredded cabbage, then dunk my kebab into any of the extra glaze before digging in. **DF, GF**

KEBABS

1½ pounds ground lamb
½ small white onion, grated on a box grater (about ½ cup)
1 small jalapeño, grated on a box grater
2 garlic cloves, grated or minced
1 tablespoon grated fresh ginger
2 teaspoons kosher salt
1 teaspoon ground coriander
1 teaspoon ground turmeric

GLAZE

¾ cup fish sauce
⅓ cup tightly packed grated palm sugar or dark brown sugar
¼ cup rice vinegar
1 small shallot, minced (about ¼ cup)
1 Fresno chile, seeded and minced
½ cup chopped fresh cilantro
Juice of 1 lime

8 (10- to 11-inch) lemongrass stalks
2 to 3 tablespoons neutral oil
Cooked white rice, for serving
Shredded cabbage, for serving

Make the kebabs: In a large bowl, combine the ground lamb, onion, jalapeño, garlic, ginger, salt, coriander, and turmeric. Mix well with your hands or a spoon until evenly combined, then cover and refrigerate for at least 30 minutes or up to overnight.

Make the glaze: In a small saucepan, combine the fish sauce, palm sugar, vinegar, and ¼ cup water. Bring to a simmer over medium heat, stirring occasionally until the sugar has dissolved, about 5 minutes. Add the shallot and chile and simmer for 10 to 12 minutes more to allow the flavors to meld and reduce the glaze a bit. It's ready when it looks like warm maple syrup. Use a pastry brush dipped in water to periodically clean the edges of the pot to help avoid burning or overcaramelization. Remove from the heat and let cool to room temperature, 10 to 15 minutes, then stir in the cilantro and lime juice.

Preheat a grill to medium-high for at least 15 minutes.

Evenly divide the lamb mixture into 8 balls, then mold each portion around 6 inches of the root end of each lemongrass stalk, pressing firmly to ensure the mixture adheres well. Brush the kebabs all over with the neutral oil, then grill for 4 to 5 minutes on the first side until well caramelized. Spoon a bit of the glaze over each kebab, then flip them over and spoon a bit of glaze over the grilled side. Cook until each kebab is nicely charred and no longer pink on the inside, 3 to 4 minutes on the second side.

Transfer to a serving platter and serve piping hot, with rice, shredded cabbage, and any remaining glaze alongside.

Szechuan Steak au Poivre

SERVES 2 TO 4

I'm obsessed with the *má*, or numbing effect, of Szechuan peppercorn. I will never forget my first experience with it at the all-you-can-eat hot pot restaurant two doors down from my first apartment in San Francisco. Inspired since then, I've had so much fun incorporating Szechuan pepper into nontraditional dishes. The steak au poivre seemed like a no-brainer and was one of the first successful experiments I had. The creamy pan sauce helps cut some of the numbness and goes perfectly with Charred Green Beans with Ginger Tomato Jam (page 150). Szechuan peppercorns are easily found at Chinese markets or online, and if you can't find green peppercorns, try pink, or just use more black pepper instead. **GF**

1 tablespoon Szechuan peppercorns
1 tablespoon whole green peppercorns
1 tablespoon whole black peppercorns
2 (12- to 14-ounce) New York strip steaks
Kosher salt
2 tablespoons neutral oil
4 tablespoons (½ stick) butter
1 small shallot, minced (about ¼ cup)
½ cup Chinese cooking wine or light filtered sake
1 cup heavy cream
1 tablespoon fresh lemon juice
Flaky sea salt

In a cold small skillet, combine the Szechuan, green, and black peppercorns. Toast over medium heat until fragrant, 3 to 4 minutes. Transfer to a small dish and let cool completely, 2 to 3 minutes. Using a mortar and pestle or spice grinder, coarsely grind the toasted peppercorns into pieces roughly the size of steel-cut oats or just a bit bigger.

At least 15 minutes before cooking the steaks, remove them from the fridge and place them on a plate or baking sheet to come to room temperature. Season them generously with kosher salt and the peppercorn mixture, pressing gently to adhere to the steaks.

In a large cast-iron or other heavy-duty skillet, heat the neutral oil over medium-high heat until it ripples and the pan is smoking. Add the steaks and cook to medium-rare, 4 to 5 minutes per side (120°F to 124°F), or your desired doneness. Transfer the steaks to a cutting board or plate, tent loosely with aluminum foil, and let rest for 10 minutes.

Add 2 tablespoons of the butter and the shallot to the same skillet and cook over medium heat until softened and translucent, 2 to 3 minutes. Remove from the heat and add the wine, then return the skillet to the heat and stir, scraping up any browned bits from the bottom of the pan. Cook until the wine has reduced by at least half or up to one-fourth, 3 to 4 minutes, then reduce the heat to medium-low and pour in the cream. Bring the sauce to a low simmer and cook until it has thickened slightly and resembles the consistency of buttermilk, 5 to 7 minutes. Remove from the heat and quickly whisk in the remaining 2 tablespoons butter, the lemon juice, and a generous pinch of kosher salt.

Serve the steaks whole or sliced into ½-inch-thick slices, then arrange them on a plate or serving platter. Spoon the Szechuan peppercorn sauce over the top and along the outside of the slices, then finish with a generous pinch of flaky salt before digging in.

BREADS & SWEET TREATS

Kimchi, Cheddar, and Chive Scones

MAKES 12 SCONES

The combo of acidic kimchi and salty cheese isn't new by any means, but I distinctly remember my first time tasting it in South Korea. Standing on a bustling street corner, I ordered a plate of buttery corn topped with creamy, salty cheese and chopped spicy kimchi. When I returned from the trip, I was determined to replicate the excitement I felt on that busy street corner as time stood still for a moment—just me and the cheesy kimchi corn. After countless tests, this recipe remains one of my favorite ways to combine the two, with the pillowy scone dough being the perfect foil to let the melty cheddar and bright, funky kimchi headline this show.

---

3 cups all-purpose flour, plus more for dusting
¼ cup sugar
1 tablespoon baking powder
1½ teaspoons kosher salt
1 teaspoon gochugaru
½ teaspoon garlic powder
½ cup (1 stick) butter, diced into ½-inch cubes and thoroughly chilled
1½ cups heavy cream, plus more for brushing
1 cup ¼-inch cheddar cheese cubes
½ cup finely chopped kimchi, drained
¼ cup chopped fresh chives
Flaky sea salt
Salted butter, whipped honey, or Jalapeño Pimento Cheese Dip (page 41), for serving

Preheat the oven to 425°F. Line two baking sheets with parchment paper.

In a large bowl, whisk together the flour, sugar, baking powder, kosher salt, gochugaru, and garlic powder just to combine. Add the butter. Working with your middle finger, index finger, and thumb, smash the butter into the flour mixture with a rubbing motion until all the butter has been broken down into shards and fairly evenly sized pieces. Work quickly to keep the butter cold and make sure not to fully incorporate the butter into the flour mixture; it should look like a shaggy, loose dough, similar to what you look for when making pie dough. Add the cream, cheddar, kimchi, and chives and gently mix with your hands until the dough comes together but still looks shaggy and is fairly wet.

Dump the dough out onto a floured surface and shape into a disc about 1½ inches thick and 10 inches wide, gently smashing it in on itself until it just comes together. The dough will be fairly wet, so flour your hands and the work surface as needed to prevent sticking. Wrap the disc of dough tightly in plastic wrap and refrigerate for 30 minutes.

Use a sharp knife to cut the disc into 10 even wedges, then place them on the prepared baking sheets. Gently brush the tops with a bit of cream and sprinkle with flaky salt. Bake both trays at once for 12 to 15 minutes, until the edges are evenly golden brown, the cheese is melty, and the dough is just barely set all the way through. Rotate the position of the pans in the oven after 9 to 10 minutes to ensure even baking.

Serve warm, with a big dollop of butter, whipped honey, or pimento cheese dip.

Seeded Flatbreads

MAKES 8 TO 10

Serve these flatbreads warm alongside anything from the Spicy Seeded Avocado Dip (page 33), Lemongrass Lamb Kebabs with Sweet Fish Sauce Glaze (page 228), Baked Cod with Muhammara and Sumac Onions (page 196) or the Green Eggs in Purgatory (page 183), and you're in for a real treat. The smattering of seeds provides a wonderful texture while the yogurt gives just the right amount of tang. VEG

- ½ cup warm water (100° to 110°F)
- 1 tablespoon honey or light brown sugar
- 1 (¼-ounce) packet active dry yeast (2¼ teaspoons)
- ½ cup plain full-fat Greek yogurt
- 3 tablespoons olive oil, plus more for greasing
- 1 large egg
- 2½ cups all-purpose flour, plus more for dusting
- 1 teaspoon kosher salt
- 2 tablespoons white sesame seeds
- 2 tablespoons poppy seeds
- 1 tablespoon cumin seeds, gently crushed
- 1 tablespoon yellow mustard seed
- ½ cup (1 stick) butter, melted
- Flaky sea salt

In the bowl of a stand mixer, stir together the warm water and honey until the honey has dissolved, 30 to 60 seconds. Sprinkle the yeast over the water and let stand until foamy, 5 to 10 minutes. Add the yogurt, olive oil, and egg and mix with a fork or whisk to combine. Add the flour and kosher salt and place on a stand mixer fitted with a dough hook. Knead on medium-low speed for about 8 minutes, until a nice smooth dough has formed. (Kneading can also be done by hand on the counter for 10 to 12 minutes.)

Place the dough in a lightly greased bowl and cover with a damp kitchen towel or plastic wrap. Let it rise in a warm place for 1 to 1½ hours, until it has about doubled in size.

Punch down the dough and divide it into 8 to 10 equal pieces. Shape each piece into a tight ball by cupping your hand over the dough and gently moving it around in a circular motion on your work surface, applying even pressure. Cover with a clean kitchen towel or plastic wrap and let rise for 30 minutes.

Place a large cast-iron skillet or heavy-duty pan over medium heat to warm up while you roll the flatbreads. In a small bowl, combine the sesame seeds, poppy seeds, cumin, and mustard seed.

Lightly dust a work surface with flour. Use a rolling pin to flatten and shape a round or oval dough ball, about ¼ inch thick. Brush one side of the flatbread with melted butter and sprinkle it generously with the seed mixture. Press the seeds lightly into the dough with your hand or the rolling pin, then gently place the flatbread seed-side down in the hot pan. Cook for 2 to 3 minutes until evenly browned, then flip and cook for 2 to 3 minutes more, until browned and cooked through, with a tender center. Remove from the heat, quickly brush with a bit more melted butter, and finish with a generous sprinkling of flaky salt. Place the flatbread between two clean kitchen towels to keep it warm and soft while you shape and cook the remaining dough, adjusting the heat of the pan between breads so it doesn't get too hot. Serve with one of the recipes mentioned above, or store in a zip-top bag at room temperature for up to 2 days, or in the freezer for up to a month.

USA ★ 1896
Blacklock

Triple Chile Cornbread

MAKES ONE 10-INCH PAN

My grandma on my mom's side is from Nebraska, and one of her go-to recipe books (that my mom still owns!) was entitled *The Nebraska Centennial First Ladies' Cookbook*, which contained recipes submitted by first ladies throughout the Cornhusker State. This is an adaptation of the Scotch Sally Lunn recipe submitted by Mrs. Mike Corgan (her own first name wasn't provided—1940s Nebraska not being a bastion of feminism, apparently) and quickly solidified itself as a family favorite. VEG

---

10 tablespoons butter, at room temperature
1¾ cups all-purpose flour
1 tablespoon baking powder
2 teaspoons chili powder
1 teaspoon kosher salt, plus more as needed
1 cup coarse-ground yellow cornmeal
1 cup sugar
2 large eggs
½ cup sour cream
1 cup whole milk
1 (4-ounce) can diced green chiles, drained
2 jalapeños: 1 finely diced, 1 sliced into rings
Flaky sea salt
Whipped butter, for serving
Honey, for serving
Jalapeño Pimento Cheese Dip (page 41), for serving

Preheat the oven to 425°F. Grease a 10-inch cast-iron skillet with 2 tablespoons of the butter and place it in the oven to preheat.

Sift the flour, baking powder, chili powder, and salt into a medium bowl, then add the cornmeal.

In the bowl of a stand mixer fitted with the paddle attachment, cream the remaining 8 tablespoons butter and the sugar on medium-high speed until light and fluffy, about 3 minutes, scraping down the bowl every minute or so. Add the eggs one at a time, beating for about a minute after each addition, then scrape down the bowl. With the mixer on low speed, add the sour cream, then alternate adding the milk and the dry mixture in three additions and mix just until the batter comes together. Scrape down the bowl, then fold in the chiles and diced jalapeño by hand until just combined, taking care not to overmix.

Carefully remove the hot skillet from the oven. Scrape the batter into the pan and smooth the top. Top with the jalapeño slices and a generous pinch of salt. Reduce the oven temperature to 375°F and bake for 30 to 40 minutes, until the bread is golden brown and a toothpick inserted into the center comes out clean.

Let cool for 15 minutes before slicing. Sprinkle with flaky salt and serve with whipped butter and a drizzle of honey.

Queenie's Whole Wheat Honey Rolls

MAKES 12 ROLLS

This recipe is a nod to the whole wheat rolls my aunt Queenie would have at almost every dinner party growing up (along with a perfectly baked side of salmon and crisp Caesar salad!). Swapping some of the traditional all-purpose flour for whole wheat gives us a nicely balanced nuttiness that, when brushed with the salted honey butter, is the perfect dinner roll. I've utilized the Chinese method of tangzhong (a cooked flour and water paste) in these rolls, which helps them achieve a wonderful bouncy, fluffy texture. VEG

TANGZHONG

¼ cup cold water
1 tablespoon all-purpose flour

DOUGH

1 cup warm water (about 115°F)
¼ cup good-quality honey
1 (¼-ounce) packet active dry yeast (2¼ teaspoons)
1 cup whole milk, at room temperature or slightly warmer
½ cup (1 stick) salted butter, melted and cooled to room temperature, plus room-temperature butter for greasing
2 large egg yolks
4½ cups all-purpose flour, plus more as needed
1 cup whole wheat flour
2 teaspoons kosher salt
Nonstick cooking spray
1 large egg, beaten, for egg wash
Flaky sea salt

SALTED HONEY BUTTER

4 tablespoons (½ stick) butter
2 tablespoons good-quality honey
2 teaspoons kosher salt, plus more as needed

Make the tangzhong: In a small pot, whisk together the cold water and flour. Cook over medium heat, whisking continuously, until you have a thick, pastelike mixture the consistency of yogurt, 3 to 4 minutes. Scrape the paste into a small bowl, cover, and let cool completely before using, about 30 minutes. (You can make the tangzhong up to 24 hours in advance and keep it refrigerated in an airtight container.)

Make the dough: In the bowl of a stand mixer, stir together the warm water and honey until the honey has dissolved, 30 to 60 seconds. Sprinkle the yeast over the water and let stand until foamy, 5 to 10 minutes.

Add the tangzhong, milk, melted butter, and egg yolks to the mixer bowl. Fit the mixer with the dough hook and add the all-purpose flour, whole wheat flour, and salt to the wet ingredients. Mix on low speed for at least 6 minutes, but no more than 10. The dough should form a somewhat tacky ball, but shouldn't be too sticky. If it is, add more all-purpose flour in ¼-cup increments until a nice ball has formed. Lightly coat a large bowl with nonstick spray and place the dough in the bowl. Cover with plastic wrap and a clean kitchen towel and let rise in a warm place for 1 to 2 hours, or until doubled in size. (You can also pop it in the fridge overnight if you want to make the rolls the next day.)

Preheat the oven to 375°F. Liberally butter a 9 × 13-inch baking dish.

Punch down the dough and divide it into 12 equal pieces. Shape each piece into a ball by cupping your hand over the dough and gently moving it around in a circular motion,

Recipe continues

on your work surface applying even pressure. Place the dough balls in the prepared baking dish, leaving space between each. Cover with a clean kitchen towel and let rise for 30 to 45 minutes, until they are puffy and have almost doubled in size. (This second rise may take longer, depending on the dough temperature.)

Use a very sharp knife to slice a roughly 1-inch X shape into the top of each dough ball, then brush the top of each roll evenly with the egg wash and sprinkle generously with flaky sea salt.

Bake the rolls for 25 to 30 minutes, until they are golden brown on top and sound hollow when tapped.

Meanwhile, make the honey butter: In a small saucepan, combine the butter, honey, and salt. Cook over low heat until everything has melted together and the mixture is slightly bubbly, 2 to 3 minutes.

As soon as the rolls come out of the oven, brush them with the salted honey butter. Serve the rolls warm, with any leftover honey butter alongside.

Spiced Dark Chocolate Budino

WITH NUTTY CARAMEL

SERVES 6

People tell me they love my desserts and pastries because they often trend toward the less-sweet side of the spectrum, but I have to say . . . sometimes when I want dessert, I just need something rich and decadent. When you're in that same mood, this dessert is all gas, no brakes. The bitterness of the caramel and the spices infused into the chocolate keep this dessert from being cloying, but it will still satisfy even the biggest sweet tooth and is always a crowd favorite. I recommend chilling the chocolate base at least 3 hours (and ideally overnight), so plan accordingly. VEG, GF

BUDINO

6 ounces dark chocolate (60% or higher), coarsely chopped
1 teaspoon kosher salt
6 large egg yolks
¼ cup sugar
1 cup heavy cream
1 cup half-and-half
1 teaspoon pure vanilla extract, or 1 vanilla bean, split lengthwise and seeds scraped out
½ teaspoon ground cinnamon
½ teaspoon chile powder
½ teaspoon ground ginger

NUTTY CARAMEL

1 cup sugar
½ cup heavy cream
6 tablespoons (¾ stick) butter, cubed
1 teaspoon kosher salt
¼ cup chopped pecans, toasted
¼ cup chopped walnuts, toasted
¼ cup pine nuts, toasted
¼ cup roasted pepitas
2 tablespoons bourbon (optional)

Whipped cream, for serving
Flaky sea salt

Make the budino: Line a baking sheet with a damp paper towel, then place your serving vessels on top (this will prevent them from sliding). You can use tea cups, soufflé cups, small jars, or even mugs.

Place the chocolate and kosher salt in a large bowl and set it aside. In another large bowl, vigorously whisk together the egg yolks and sugar until they are slightly pale in color.

In a medium pot, combine the cream, half-and-half, vanilla (if using a vanilla bean, add both the seeds and the scraped pod), cinnamon, chile powder, and ginger. Heat over medium heat until it has come to a light simmer, about 6 to 8 minutes. Remove the vanilla pod (if using).

While whisking continuously, slowly pour the hot cream mixture into the egg yolks and whisk until well combined. Return the mixture to the pot and cook over low heat, stirring continuously with a rubber spatula to avoid curdling the eggs, until the mixture has thickened to the consistency of eggnog or crepe batter, 6 to 10 minutes.

Pour the egg mixture into the bowl with the chocolate and let stand for 3 minutes to melt the chocolate, then whisk well to fully combine. Using a ladle or measuring cup, evenly divide the budino among your serving vessels, then cover with plastic wrap and chill for at least 3 hours or up to overnight.

Recipe continues

Make the caramel: In a medium pot with a lid, combine the sugar and ½ cup water. Stir with a rubber spatula, then pop on the lid. Cook over medium heat for about 5 minutes, then take a peek. If you can still see sugar crystals, cover and cook for 2 to 3 minutes more. If the mixture is bubbling and totally clear, without any sugar granules, leave the lid off and cook without stirring until the caramel reaches a deep amber color, about 10 minutes.

Meanwhile, set the cream, butter, kosher salt, pecans, walnuts, pine nuts, pepitas, and bourbon (if using) near the stove.

When the caramel is dark amber, turn off the heat and carefully pour in half the cream. (It will bubble and spit, so take care!) Stir to fully incorporate, then add the remaining cream and stir to combine. Add the butter, pecans, walnuts, pine nuts, pepitas, bourbon (if using), and kosher salt and stir well until the butter is totally melted into the caramel. Let cool until just barely warm before serving, 15 to 20 minutes.

Remove the plastic wrap from the budino, then top each one with a generous amount of the barely warm nutty caramel. (Any leftover caramel can be stored in an airtight container or jar in the fridge for up to 2 weeks.) Top with whipped cream and a pinch of flaky salt just before digging in.

Toasted Rice Pudding

WITH LIMEY MANGO AND CRUNCHY COCONUT

SERVES 4 TO 6

Is rice pudding already one of the coziest desserts of all time? Absolutely. Does that mean we can't try to amp it up even more? Absolutely not. By toasting the fragrant basmati rice and butter to a nutty golden brown, we get a result that is pure cashmere. Topped with tart, lime-marinated mangoes and crunchy coconut, this rice pudding is the perfectly balanced post-dinner treat. **VEG**

CRUNCHY COCONUT

½ cup all-purpose flour
¼ cup unsweetened coconut flakes
4 tablespoons (½ stick) butter, melted
¼ cup sliced almonds
3 tablespoons packed dark brown sugar
Small pinch of kosher salt

RICE PUDDING

5 tablespoons butter
¾ cup uncooked basmati rice
1 teaspoon grated fresh ginger
2 cups whole milk, plus more as needed
1 (14-ounce) can evaporated milk
¼ cup granulated sugar
1 vanilla bean, split lengthwise and seeds scraped out, or 1 teaspoon vanilla paste
½ teaspoon kosher salt
⅛ teaspoon ground cinnamon

LIMEY MANGOES

2 ripe large mangoes, chopped into ½-inch chunks
Zest and juice of 1 lime
1 tablespoon coconut-flavored rum (optional)
1 tablespoon honey
¼ cup torn fresh Thai or opal basil leaves

Make the coconut: Preheat the oven to 350°F. Line a small baking sheet with parchment paper or aluminum foil.

In a small bowl, stir together the flour, coconut flakes, melted butter, almonds, brown sugar, and salt until well combined. Crumble this mixture onto the prepared baking sheet into an even layer. Bake for 10 minutes, then remove from the oven and stir well. Bake for 5 to 10 minutes more, until the mixture is very aromatic, a medium golden brown, and crisp all the way through, almost like a granola. Remove from the oven and let cool.

Make the pudding: In a large heavy-bottomed pot or Dutch oven, combine 3 tablespoons of the butter and the rice. Cook over medium-high heat, stirring frequently, to evenly toast the rice and let the butter brown, 3 to 5 minutes. Add the ginger and cook, stirring continuously, for another minute or so, until fragrant. Add the whole milk, evaporated milk, granulated sugar, vanilla seeds, salt, and cinnamon and stir well, then reduce the heat to low. Cook, stirring every 5 minutes to make sure the bottom doesn't scorch, until the rice is cooked but not mushy and the pudding has the consistency of oatmeal, 30 to 40 minutes. If the rice isn't tender enough but the pudding is getting too thick, add a bit more milk. Add the remaining 2 tablespoons butter to the hot rice pudding and stir until completely melted.

Meanwhile, make the mangoes: In a small bowl, stir together the mangoes, lime zest, lime juice, rum (if using), and honey. Set aside to marinate for at least 15 minutes, or up to 2 hours.

Divide the pudding into serving bowls, then top with a generous helping of the marinated mangoes, the crunchy coconut, and basil. I like this rice pudding best served hot, but if you want to serve it cold, place into a shallow container and chill, covered, in the fridge until completely cooled (about 2 hours, or overnight), then divide into glasses for serving. You may need to adjust the consistency with a bit of milk, as it will firm up as it chills. Store any leftover rice pudding in the fridge for up to 5 days.

Feeling a little bit EXTRA?

Make your own jam—the recipe is on page 250! Homemade strawberry jam will give you the most gorgeous bright pink color in the frosting and you'll even have some extra to shmear on toast the next morning!

Poppy Seed Meyer Lemon Buttermilk Cookies

WITH STRAWBERRY FROSTING

MAKES 16 TO 18 COOKIES

My grandma Shirley passed down two recipes to my mom that we baked all the time growing up—her lemon poppy seed cake and her buttermilk sugar cookies. This mash-up of the two recipes is my greedy attempt at cramming all the luxuriousness of the two recipes into one single Frankencookie. The Meyer lemon tree outside my childhood home is an absolute machine and produces fruit year-round, so it was easy to snag a few lemons right off the tree whenever I needed them for my baking projects. If you can't get your hands on Meyers, conventional lemons will do the trick and I find making your own strawberry jam (recipe follows) will give the frosting the best flavor and color! **VEG**

COOKIE DOUGH

- 3½ cups all-purpose flour, plus more for dusting
- ½ cup cornstarch
- ½ teaspoon baking soda
- ½ teaspoon kosher salt
- 1½ cups granulated sugar
- 1 cup (2 sticks) butter, at room temperature
- 1 teaspoon pure vanilla extract or vanilla bean paste
- Zest of 1 Meyer lemon
- 2 large eggs
- ½ cup buttermilk
- ¼ cup poppy seeds

FROSTING

- 3 cups powdered sugar
- 2 tablespoons strawberry jam, homemade (recipe follows) or store-bought
- 2 tablespoons butter, at room temperature
- ¼ teaspoon pure vanilla extract or vanilla bean paste

Make the dough: Sift the flour, cornstarch, baking soda, and salt into a medium bowl.

In the bowl of a stand mixer fitted with the paddle attachment, combine the granulated sugar, butter, vanilla, and lemon zest. Beat on medium-high speed for 1 to 2 minutes. Scrape down the bowl, then beat on medium-high until the mixture is fluffy-looking and pale in color, 1 minute more. Add the eggs one at a time, mixing for 1 minute after each addition. Scrape the bowl down again and beat for 1 minute more, until well combined and fluffy. Scrape down the bowl, then add the flour mixture. With the mixer running on low speed, slowly drizzle in the buttermilk and mix just until the flour and buttermilk are fully incorporated.

Dump the dough out onto a lightly floured work surface and shape it into a log roughly 3 inches in diameter and 10 to 12 inches long. Very lightly flour the dough as needed to prevent sticking, but try to avoid using too much, and brush off any excess. (The dough should be soft but easy to work with—if you find it's not cooperating, cover it well and refrigerate for 30 minutes before finishing the shaping.)

Lay out a piece of parchment paper that's long enough to wrap the log and sprinkle it with the poppy seeds. Roll the log in the poppy seeds, lightly pressing them into the dough as you roll, until the log is completely covered. (If the seeds aren't sticking, there may be too much flour on the dough—brush off any excess and try

Recipe continues

again.) Tightly roll up the log in the parchment and freeze for at least 30 minutes, or up to overnight.

Make the frosting: In a large bowl, combine the powdered sugar, jam, butter, and vanilla. Use a sturdy spatula or wooden spoon to incorporate. If the frosting looks too thick, thin it by adding water 1 tablespoon at a time, fully incorporating each addition before adding more. The finished product should have the consistency of canned frosting. Cover the bowl while you bake the cookies.

Preheat the oven to 325°F. Line two baking sheets with parchment paper.

Using a sharp knife, cut the dough into rounds about ½ inch thick, then place them on the prepared baking sheets, spacing them evenly. If you cut off the butt ends, you should end up with 16 to 18 cookies.

Bake for 12 minutes, then swap the positions of the pans on the racks and bake for 6 to 8 minutes more, until the cookies are pale, soft, and just barely set to the touch. Let cool on the baking sheets for 10 minutes, then transfer the cookies to a wire rack to cool completely, 15 to 20 minutes.

Dollop 1 to 2 tablespoons of the frosting onto each cooled cookie and use a spoon or offset spatula to spread it evenly. Let the frosting set for 30 minutes before enjoying. The cookies can be stored in an airtight container or zip-top bag at room temperature for up to 3 days.

Homemade Strawberry Jam

MAKES ABOUT 1½ CUPS

- 2 cups diced very ripe strawberries
- ¼ cup sugar
- 1 tablespoon fresh lemon juice
- 1 teaspoon vanilla bean paste or pure vanilla extract

In a small pot, combine the strawberries, sugar, lemon juice, vanilla, and ¼ cup water. Bring to a boil over medium-high heat, stirring frequently, then reduce the heat to medium-low and cook the mixture down to a nice thick, syrupy consistency, 12 to 15 minutes. The jam should be glossy and vibrant red in color.

Scoop the jam into a heatproof airtight container, cover, and refrigerate until cooled completely before using, about 30 minutes. Store in the refrigerator for up to 2 weeks.

Black Sesame Tahini Swirl Cake

WITH SAUTÉED CHERRIES

MAKES 1 LOAF CAKE

I understand how intimidating baking cakes can be, but the only way to get better at any craft is by practicing. This cake is a great set of training wheels for those first learning to bake. Oil-based cakes like this one are more forgiving and moist than butter-based cakes, plus they have the added benefit of *not* relying on stand mixers. This cake has a huge effort-to-reward ratio; it comes together with minimal effort (okay, as far as cakes are concerned). Serve just barely warm with these jammy sauteéd cherries and your guests will think you're a seasoned baking pro—I promise! **VEG**

SESAME SWIRL BASE

Nonstick cooking spray
¼ cup black sesame seeds
1 tablespoon sugar
1 tablespoon all-purpose flour
Small pinch of kosher salt

BATTER

1¾ cups all-purpose flour
1 teaspoon baking powder
¾ teaspoon kosher salt
1¼ cups sugar
2 large eggs
1 teaspoon pure vanilla extract
½ teaspoon toasted sesame oil
¾ cup whole milk
¼ cup plus 2 tablespoons tahini
¼ cup plus 2 tablespoons neutral oil
1 tablespoon black sesame seeds

Preheat the oven to 325°F. Coat a 9 × 5-inch loaf pan with cooking spray. You can line the pan with parchment paper as well, if you like.

Make the sesame swirl base: In a small food processor or blender, combine the sesame seeds, sugar, flour, and salt. Process until the sesame seeds are ground into a fine powder, 2 to 3 minutes. Transfer to a small bowl.

Make the batter: Sift together the flour, baking powder, and salt into a medium bowl.

In a large bowl, whisk together the sugar, eggs, vanilla, and sesame oil until light and fluffy. Add the milk, tahini, and neutral oil and whisk to combine well. Add the flour mixture to the egg mixture and whisk just until all the lumps are gone, taking care not to overmix.

Remove ½ cup of the batter and stir it into the sesame swirl base until well combined. Transfer the sesame swirl batter to a piping bag. (You can also use a zip-top bag, or just use a spoon instead of piping.)

Pour half the light-colored batter into the prepared pan, then pipe or spoon half the sesame swirl batter evenly over the light batter. Repeat with the remaining light batter, then the remaining sesame swirl batter. Use a knife or toothpick to gently swirl the batter a few times. Sprinkle the sesame seeds over the top of the cake, then bake for 1 hour to 1 hour 15 minutes, until the top is golden

Recipe and ingredients continue

SAUTÉED CHERRIES

2 tablespoons butter
1 teaspoon toasted sesame oil
1 pound ripe red cherries, pitted (halved, if large)
¼ cup sugar
1 tablespoon honey
2 tablespoons Cointreau or other orange liqueur

Whipped cream or crème fraîche, for serving (optional)

brown and a toothpick inserted into the center comes out clean. Let cool in the pan on a wire rack for 15 minutes, then remove from the pan and let cool on a wire rack for 15 to 25 minutes more.

Meanwhile, make the cherries: In a medium sauté pan, heat the butter and sesame oil over medium-high heat until the butter is melted and bubbling. Add the cherries, sugar, and honey and cook, stirring frequently, until the mixture is syrupy and all the sugar granules have dissolved, about 5 minutes.

Remove from the heat, add the Cointreau, then set the pan over high heat, dipping one corner of the pan toward the flame to ignite the alcohol (alternatively, ignite them carefully with a match or small blowtorch). Cook just until the flames die off, then remove from the heat. The cherries should be cooked down but not mushy.

Slice the cake into 8 to 10 slices and serve slightly warm with a generous helping of the cherries, their luscious sauce, and a dollop of whipped cream or crème fraîche, if desired.

Peanut Butter Affogato Sundaes

MAKES 6 SUNDAES

We're taking some inspiration from my viral Shaken Peanut Butter Espresso here, folks. While the beverage itself is top-tier, I thought it was only right to make it *a little bit extra* by turning it into a luxurious dessert of peanut buttery fudge sauce, cocoa whipped cream, and hot espresso. **VEG, GF**

PEANUT BUTTER FUDGE SAUCE

3 ounces 70% dark chocolate, coarsely chopped
2 tablespoons smooth peanut butter
1 tablespoon butter
1½ cups heavy cream
1 tablespoon powdered sugar
1 teaspoon pure vanilla extract
½ teaspoon kosher salt

COCOA WHIPPED CREAM

1 cup heavy cream
2 tablespoons unsweetened dark cocoa powder
2 tablespoons powdered sugar
1 teaspoon pure vanilla extract
Small pinch of kosher salt

FOR SERVING

6 large scoops of your favorite ice cream
½ cup crushed roasted peanuts
Flaky sea salt
6 shots of espresso

Make the sauce: Place the chocolate, peanut butter, and butter in a medium bowl.

In a small pot, combine the cream, powdered sugar, vanilla, and kosher salt. Bring to a simmer over medium heat, stirring to dissolve the sugar, then pour the cream mixture over the chocolate mixture. Let stand for 5 minutes to melt the chocolate, then whisk until the sauce is well emulsified and glossy.

Make the cream: In a medium bowl, combine the cream, cocoa powder, powdered sugar, vanilla, and kosher salt. Whisk or beat with a handheld mixer on high speed until the mixture holds stiff peaks, 3 to 4 minutes. Refrigerate until ready to serve.

Divide the peanut butter fudge sauce among six serving vessels (I like to use vintage tea cups, martini glasses, or cute ceramic dessert bowls). Place a large scoop of ice cream on top of the fudge sauce, then add a big dollop of the cocoa whipped cream. Sprinkle crushed peanuts and flaky salt over the whip.

Right before serving, pour a shot of espresso into each serving vessel and devour immediately as the espresso melts into the luscious fudge sauce.

Make your own peanut butter ice cream—the recipe is on the next page!

Silky Peanut Butter Ice Cream

MAKES ABOUT 1 QUART

3 cups half-and-half
1 teaspoon vanilla bean paste or pure vanilla extract
½ teaspoon kosher salt
6 egg yolks
½ cup lightly packed light brown sugar
¼ cup granulated sugar
¾ cup smooth peanut butter
¼ teaspoon ice cream stabilizer (optional)

In a medium saucepan, stir together the half-and-half, vanilla, and salt. Heat over medium heat until warm but not boiling.

In a large bowl, whisk together the egg yolks, brown sugar, and granulated sugar until pale and slightly fluffy. While whisking continuously, slowly drizzle the warm half-and-half mixture into the egg mixture, then whisk until well combined. Return the mixture to the saucepan and cook over medium heat, stirring continuously with a wooden spoon or spatula, until the mixture thickens enough to coat the back of the spoon (it should have the consistency of buttermilk), 5 to 7 minutes. Take care not to let it boil! Remove from the heat and whisk in peanut butter and ice cream stabilizer (if using) until the ice cream base is fully combined and smooth. Let cool to room temperature, 30 to 45 minutes, then refrigerate for at least 2 hours or until completely chilled.

Pour the chilled ice cream base into an ice cream maker and churn according to the manufacturer's instructions until it reaches a soft-serve consistency. Transfer the ice cream to an airtight container and freeze for at least 4 hours or until firm before serving. The ice cream will keep in your freezer for up to a month.

Blue Ribbon Peach and Cardamom Pie

MAKES 1 LARGE PIE

The first cooking competition I ever entered, and won, was at the Santa Cruz County Fair when I was all of eleven years old. The county fair was something of a family affair—my mom also entered her poetry and won a few blue ribbons herself. (My dad called these county fair contests the "Hillbilly Olympics"—I think he was just envious he never won a ribbon of his own!) My winning entry was a peach pie with a lattice top, stuffed with peaches I had plucked from the tree in our backyard the day before. I'll never forget the look on the face of the granny who took my entry back to the judges. Her proud grin was all the prize I needed that day! Despite their best efforts, the team of judges couldn't quite put their finger on the secret ingredient . . . can you guess which one won me the blue ribbon? **VEG**

CRUST

- 2 cups all-purpose flour, plus more for dusting
- 2 tablespoons packed light brown sugar
- 1 teaspoon kosher salt
- Zest of ½ lemon
- ¾ cup (1½ sticks) butter, cut into ½-inch cubes and thoroughly chilled
- ½ cup iced black tea, vodka, or water, plus more as needed

FILLING

- 3 pounds fresh or frozen peaches (pitted and sliced if fresh)
- ½ cup packed light brown sugar
- 6 tablespoons (¾ stick) butter, melted
- 2 tablespoons cornstarch
- 2 tablespoons all-purpose flour
- ½ teaspoon ground cardamom (freshly ground, if possible)
- ½ teaspoon ground cinnamon
- 1 vanilla bean, split lengthwise and seeds scraped out, or 1 teaspoon pure vanilla extract
- Zest of ½ lemon
- 1 tablespoon fresh lemon juice
- Small pinch of kosher salt

Make the crust: In a large bowl, combine the flour, brown sugar, salt, and lemon zest. Add the butter cubes and use your fingers to smash the butter into the dry ingredients, forming shards somewhere between the size of a pea and a nickel. Work quickly and don't break the butter down too much so it doesn't get too warm. Add the tea and gently work it in with your hands until the dough just barely comes together. If the dough is too crumbly, add a bit more tea, 1 tablespoon at a time. Shape the dough into a disc, wrap it in plastic wrap, and refrigerate for at least 30 minutes. The crust can be made ahead and stored in the fridge for up to 2 days.

Make the filling: In a large bowl, combine the peaches, brown sugar, melted butter, cornstarch, flour, lemon zest, lemon juice, cardamom, cinnamon, vanilla seeds, and salt. Gently toss to coat the peaches evenly.

Make the crumble: In a medium bowl, combine the flour, granulated sugar, brown sugar, cardamom, salt, and cinnamon. Add the butter and use your fingers to blend until the mixture resembles coarse crumbs, completely working the butter into the dry mixture; no chunks of butter should be left. You want a crumbly, irregular mixture.

Position a rack in the bottom third of the oven and preheat to 375°F.

On a lightly floured surface, roll out the chilled dough to fit your pie pan. The

Recipe and ingredients continue

CRUMBLE

1¼ cups all-purpose flour
¼ cup granulated sugar
¼ cup lightly packed dark brown sugar
1 teaspoon ground cardamom (freshly ground, if possible)
1 teaspoon kosher salt
½ teaspoon ground cinnamon
¾ cup (1½ sticks) butter, cut into ½-inch cubes and thoroughly chilled

dough should be roughly ⅛ inch thick. Carefully transfer the dough to a 9- or 10-inch deep-dish pie pan, tucking it down into the corners, and trim any dough hanging over the edge, leaving about 1 inch of excess. Fold the excess in on itself, then use your fingers or a fork to crimp the edge as you like.

Pour the peach filling into the prepared crust, spreading it evenly. Sprinkle the crumble mixture evenly over the filling. Bake the pie for 1 hour 15 minutes to 1 hour 30 minutes, until the crumble is golden brown, the filling is bubbling, and the edges of the pie are a deep, rich golden color. (If the edges of the crust start to brown too quickly, cover them with foil to prevent burning.)

Let cool completely, about 2 hours, before slicing into the pie and seeing if your friends can guess the secret spice that won me a blue ribbon! You can make the pie the day before, then gently warm it in a 325°F oven for 10 minutes before serving the next day. Leftover pie can be kept covered on the counter for up to 2 days or in the fridge for up to 5 days.

THEE Chocolate Chunk Cookie

MAKES 14 TO 16 COOKIES

Does the world need another chocolate chip (okay, chip + chunk) recipe? Absolutely. Here's me putting my name in the hat for the best CCC recipe of all time. The combo of the chips and chunks along with the nutty malted milk make for a clear winner. VEG

2¾ cups all-purpose flour
¼ cup malted milk powder
1½ teaspoons kosher salt
1 teaspoon baking powder
½ teaspoon baking soda
1 cup (2 sticks) butter, at room temperature
1 cup packed dark brown sugar
¾ cup granulated sugar
2 teaspoons pure vanilla extract
2 large eggs, at room temperature
1 large egg yolk, at room temperature
8 ounces dark chocolate chips
9 ounces dark chocolate, chopped into chunks up to ½ inch
Flaky sea salt

Feeling a little bit EXTRA?

For a professional-looking finish to your cookies, hold back a small handful of the chocolate chips. After you've scooped the cookies and sprinkled them with salt, dot the top of each cookie with a few chips, then chill and continue as directed. Once baked, this gives a super-inviting, melty, and textured look to the cookies!

Line two baking sheets with parchment paper or silicone baking mats.

In a medium bowl, whisk together the flour, malted milk powder, kosher salt, baking powder, and baking soda.

In the bowl of a stand mixer fitted with the paddle attachment, combine the butter, brown sugar, granulated sugar, and vanilla and beat on high speed until light and fluffy, 3 to 4 minutes. Add the eggs and egg yolk one at a time, mixing until fully incorporated after each addition. Scrape down the bowl. Add the dry ingredients, chocolate chips, and chopped dark chocolate and mix on low speed until just combined.

Using a cookie scoop or spoon, portion the dough into tangerine-size balls and place them on the prepared baking sheets, leaving some space between them. Roll each dough ball into a nice round shape, then dip the top in a generous amount of flaky salt and return them to the baking sheets. Refrigerate the dough balls for at least 30 minutes or ideally overnight.

Preheat the oven to 350°F.

Bake two trays of the cookies for 16 to 20 minutes, until the edges are golden brown and the centers are set but still slightly soft. Rotate the pan positions in the oven after 12 minutes to get the most even bake. (I always take my cookies out *just* before I think they're actually done.) Let cool on the baking sheets for 5 minutes, then transfer the cookies to a wire rack to cool completely, 15 to 20 minutes. Store any leftover cookies (as if!) in an airtight container at room temperature for up to 3 days. You can also freeze the unbaked dough balls in a zip-top bag for up to 1 month; place the frozen dough balls on lined baking sheets and let stand at room temperature for 30 minutes before baking.

Grandma Gruen's Molasses Cake

WITH ORANGE-SCENTED WHIP

MAKES ONE 9-INCH ROUND

We have about ten family birthdays in quick succession during late fall/early winter, and this was the cake served at every. single. one. of our parties. The warming spices and rich molasses coalesce into the perfect nostalgic treat for those cooler months. I like to glaze the cake a few hours in advance to let it set up and get a bit crunchy. We usually ate this with vanilla ice cream, but I now prefer it with this orange-scented whip with just a bit of booze. VEG

CAKE

1 tablespoon butter, at room temperature
1½ cups all-purpose flour, plus more for dusting
1 cup blackstrap molasses
½ cup vegetable shortening
½ cup boiling water
1 teaspoon baking soda
½ teaspoon ground cinnamon
½ teaspoon ground nutmeg
½ teaspoon ground allspice
½ teaspoon kosher salt
1 large egg
1 teaspoon pure vanilla extract

ORANGE-SCENTED WHIP

1 cup heavy cream
2 tablespoons granulated sugar
Zest of ½ orange
1 tablespoon fresh orange juice
1 tablespoon Cointreau or Grand Marnier
⅛ teaspoon ground cinnamon

GLAZE

2 cups powdered sugar, sifted
½ cup unsweetened cocoa powder
Pinch of kosher salt
2 to 4 tablespoons whole milk

Make the cake: Preheat the oven to 325°F. Grease a 9-inch cake pan with the butter, then lightly dust with 1 tablespoon of flour, shaking it around and tapping out any excess.

Place the molasses and shortening in a medium bowl and pour the boiling water over them, stirring gently to fully melt.

Sift together the flour, baking soda, cinnamon, nutmeg, allspice, and salt into a large bowl, then add the egg and vanilla. Mix gently with a wooden spoon. While stirring, slowly drizzle in the water-shortening mixture and stir just until the batter has come together and there are no lumps, taking care not to overmix. Pour the batter into the prepared pan and smooth the top with a spatula.

Bake on the middle rack for 35 minutes, or until a toothpick inserted into the cake comes out clean. Invert the cake onto a wire rack and remove the pan. Let cool completely before glazing, about 30 minutes to an hour.

Make the whip: In a large bowl, combine the cream, granulated sugar, orange zest, orange juice, Cointreau, and cinnamon. Whisk until the cream holds stiff peaks, about 5 minutes. Cover and refrigerate up to 4 hours in advance.

Make the glaze: In a large bowl, whisk together the powdered sugar, cocoa powder, and salt, then slowly add the milk, whisking until you have a glaze with the consistency of Nutella.

Transfer the cooled cake to a serving dish and liberally glaze the top, letting the glaze drip down the sides. (I like to glaze the cake a few hours before serving to give it ample time to set, leaving a nice crunchy crust on the outside and a soft, melty texture on the inside.)

Slice the cake and serve with a large dollop of the orange-scented whip.

Kettle Corn Crème Brûlée

SERVES 6

I love coming back to a little salty nibble after my dessert, but with this riff off classic crème brûlée, we get the best of both worlds! A luxurious, smooth custard with a hint of nuttiness from the steeped popcorn, topped with a textural delight—caramelized crunchy sugar. I like to serve mine with extra kettle corn on the side, but hey, I'm extra like that. VEG, GF

2 tablespoons neutral oil
⅓ cup popcorn kernels
½ cup plus 1 tablespoon granulated sugar
2 cups heavy cream, plus more as needed
1 cup half-and-half, plus more as needed
1 vanilla bean, split lengthwise and seeds scraped out, or 1 tablespoon vanilla bean paste
7 large egg yolks
½ teaspoon kosher salt
About ½ cup raw or turbinado sugar

In a large Dutch oven or heavy stainless-steel pot with a lid, heat the neutral oil over medium-high heat until it ripples and is just barely starting to smoke, 2 to 3 minutes. Add the popcorn kernels and shake the pot to coat each kernel well. Cook, shaking the pot continuously, until the first kernel pops, then quickly sprinkle the kernels with 1 tablespoon of the granulated sugar. Cover and cook, still shaking the pot continuously, until the popping stops, 2 to 3 minutes, then remove from the heat.

Add the cream, half-and-half, and vanilla (if you're using a vanilla bean, add the seeds and the scraped pod) to the pot with the popcorn (remove a few small handfuls of popped kernels for garnish first). Cook over low heat, stirring now and then, for 25 to 30 minutes to infuse the popcorn into the cream.

Meanwhile, in a medium bowl, whisk together the egg yolks, remaining ½ cup granulated sugar, and salt until combined.

Preheat the oven to 300°F. Fill a large roasting pan with hot water and place it on the bottom of the oven.

Strain the cream mixture through a fine-mesh sieve into a large bowl or 4-cup measuring cup. You need exactly 3 cups of the cream mixture; add a touch more cream or half-and-half to get to the 3-cup mark as needed.

While whisking continuously, pour the cream mixture into the egg mixture and whisk until the custard is well combined.

Place 6 (8-ounce) ramekins on a baking sheet and evenly distribute the custard among the ramekins. Bake for 30 to 40 minutes, until just barely set but still wobbling quite a bit in the middle. Let cool for 30 minutes, then cover and refrigerate for at least 3 hours or ideally overnight.

Sprinkle each ramekin with 1 to 2 tablespoons of the raw sugar, then brûlée the sugar with a torch until well caramelized. Working in small, tight circles with the flame will give you the best results! Serve each crème brûlée with a small handful of kettle corn on top or on the side, for garnish.

Acknowledgments

Ryan (and Odie), I can't thank you enough for the love and support in this endeavor and for letting me turn our home into a studio for recipe development, photo shoots, video filming, and cooking content—it was not a small act and your trust in me allowed me to produce an incredible cookbook.

Amanda Bernardi and the entire team at Highline, thank you for making this opportunity possible, for always seeing the vision, and for talking me down whenever the imposter syndrome tried to take hold.

Caitlin, your patience working with someone who is by no means a writer has been inspiring. Thanks to you and everyone at Union Square & Co.—Amanda Englander, Ivy McFadden, Renée Bollier, Lisa Forde—for going on this journey with me.

To the most badass crew of women who helped turn every written recipe into an inviting, elegant world within each photo: Sebira, Erin, Jillian, and Tina. You are all so beautifully talented and such a treat to work with. Our time together in the studio still feels like a dream to me. How did I get so lucky?!

I'm indebted to my brother Sam who spent countless hours reading recipes and revising my writing with me. Love you, brother.

My amazing team of recipe testers—Charlie, Lydia, Maddie, Robin, Kate, and Sam. These recipes are the polished gems they are because of all the work you put into testing them.

A massive thank you to Citarella Gourmet Market for their contributions to making sure I was stocked for the photo shoot with some of the freshest seafood I've ever used. I can always count on y'all!

My mentor from day one, Randy Torres, who has always trusted me and made me the cook I am today—none of my success would be possible without you.

Cheralee, your knowledge and excitement has guided many of the decisions I have made, not only with this book but with my career as a whole. Thank you for all the inspiration and all the entertaining voice memos along the way.

Ashley, Jared, and all the IKONICFOX family—I am so proud to be a part of this incredibly talented, driven group of individuals. Thank you for guiding me through this and rolling the dice with me since day one!

Para mi guía en la cocina desde siempre, Lucy. Gracias por compartir tus recetas, tus memorias, y tu amor.

And finally, I need to thank my beautiful parents, Charlie and Gail, whose support of me has been unwavering in all aspects of my life. I am proud of the man that I am today because you made the sacrifices in your life to make me this way. Thank you for giving me every opportunity to make this dreamy life I have possible.

Index

D

E

F

G

Q

R

S